CHILD ABUSE
AND THE
CRIMINAL JUSTICE
SYSTEM

D1570575

David A. Schultz and Christina DeJong
General Editors

Vol. 9

PETER LANG
New York • Washington, D.C./Baltimore • Bern
Frankfurt am Main • Berlin • Brussels • Vienna • Oxford

Kimberly A. McCabe

CHILD ABUSE
AND THE
CRIMINAL
JUSTICE SYSTEM

PETER LANG
New York • Washington, D.C./Baltimore • Bern
Frankfurt am Main • Berlin • Brussels • Vienna • Oxford

Library of Congress Cataloging-in-Publication Data

McCabe, Kimberly A.
Child abuse and the criminal justice system / Kimberly A. McCabe.
p. cm. — (Studies in crime and punishment; vol. 9)
Includes bibliographical references and index.
1. Child abuse—United States. 2. Criminal justice,
Administration of—United States. I. Title. II. Series.
HV6626.52 .M33 364.15'554'0973—dc21 2002034022
ISBN 0-8204-5786-8
ISSN 1529-2444

Bibliographic information published by **Die Deutsche Bibliothek**.
Die Deutsche Bibliothek lists this publication in the 'Deutsche
Nationalbibliografie'; detailed bibliographic data is available
on the Internet at http://dnb.ddb.de

Cover design by Lisa Barfield

The paper in this book meets the guidelines for permanence and durability
of the Committee on Production Guidelines for Book Longevity
of the Council of Library Resources.

For Jessica and Mac

Contents

CHAPTER 1

A History of
Child Abuse

On December 26, 1996, when the body of 5-year-old Jon-Benét Ramsey was discovered in the basement of her family's 15-room house in Colorado, the murder of a child in the safety of her home and the assertions by the media of a possible case of child abuse became very real and very public problems for America. Whether the murderer of Jon-Benét Ramsey was a stranger or a family member, we may never know, and, with the dismissal of the grand jury in October of 1999, the search for the truth will probably be simply an expensive exercise in futility (O'Driscoll, 1999). In June of 2002, with the Utah disappearance of Elizabeth Smart and the media's portrayal of her father as a man with a secret life of sexual exploits, the topic of child abuse surfaced again.

Historically, our society has been concerned about child abuse to varying degrees. In most instances, we prefer to view abuse within the home as simply a family problem. This view was supported in DeShaney v. Winnebago County Department of Social Services (1989). In this case, the court decided that the State had no constitutional duty to protect a young boy from physical abuse by his father although the department had received reports of possible abuse. However, once child abuse cases are reported and seized upon by the media, we then wish to act quickly to end child abuse. Hence, like many other areas of concern for the criminal justice system, child abuse or rather the prevention of child abuse has historically received reactive efforts rather than proactive efforts by the system.

Law enforcement data indicate that nearly 6% of all U.S. victims of violent crime are under the age of 12 (Wilson, 2000). In addition, in approximately one-third of the sexual assaults reported to police, the victims are under the age of 12 (Wilson, 2000). From 1986 to 1993, the number of cases of abused and neglected children reported to U.S. law enforcement agencies doubled to nearly 1.6 million cases (Sedlak & Broadhurst, 1996). In 1996, it was estimated that more than 3 million children were victims of child abuse and/or neglect (Brownstein, 2000). Girls were sexually abused at three times the rate of boys, but boys were more often victims of emotional neglect and physical abuse than girls (Sedlak & Broadhurst, 1996). Based upon data reported to law enforcement and available through the National Incident Based Reporting System (NIBRS), 40% of sexual assaults and 42% of physical assaults on children involved victims under the age of 8 (Finkelhor & Ormrod, 2001). In addition, an estimated 2,000 children die as a result of either child abuse or neglect each year in the United States (Langstaff & Sleeper, 2001) with at least three children dying every day as result of parental maltreatment (Kelley, Thornberry & Smith, 1997). Despite these alarming figures and efforts to educate the public on the subject and aggressively target those who abuse children, there are those who suggest that we are no closer to ending child abuse in this country than we were over a century ago when the first case of child abuse was reported.

Child Abuse Defined

Children are abused and neglected by parents, grandparents, siblings, and others outside of the family. The phenomenon of what we call "child abuse" existed yesterday, exists today, and is expected to continue long after the readers and writer of this text are deceased. Children's life experiences shape their adulthoods. If tomorrow's leaders are to be strong, thoughtful individuals, their upbringing should be one of love and support; however, researchers in the area of child abuse and neglect now know that many children never have the opportunities afforded to them by a loving family environment.

The term *child abuse* refers to victimizations that are generally divided into the four categories of: (1) physical abuse (2) sexual abuse (3) emotional abuse, and (4) neglect. Children may be the victims of one type or all four types of abuse; thus, child abuse rarely refers to a mutually exclusive category of abuse.

A Historical Perspective on Child Abuse

Dating back to the Bible, stories of child abuse include not only sexual and physical abuse but also the killing of children. In the Old Testament, Abraham intended to sacrifice his son Isaac, and, in Egypt, the pharaoh ordered the death of all male

KEY TERMS IN THE DEFINITION OF CHILD ABUSE

Physical Abuse—the nonaccidental injury of a child or children inflicted by a person (Crosson-Tower, 1999). Physical abuse ranges in severity from a spanking that results in minor bruises to a beating that results in the hospitalization of the child.

Sexual Abuse—the sexual exploitation of or sexual activities with a child or children (Wallace, 1999). The sexual abuse of a child (as "child" is defined by state jurisdictional law) includes but is not limited to vaginal intercourse, oral sex, sodomy, and

(Key Terms continued) the production and distribution of child pornography.

Emotional Abuse—a pattern of psychologically destructive behavior targeted toward a child or children (Garbarino, Guttman & Seeley, 1986). Included under the category of emotional abuse are isolating, terrorizing, ignoring, and corrupting the child (Crosson-Tower, 1999).

Neglect—a caretaker fails to provide for the child's basic needs of survival (Bartollas, 2000). Child neglect may be in but is not limited to the areas of supervision, physical care, emotional care, and education.

infants; hence, the story states that Moses was placed in a basket and floated down a stream. It would be absurd for us to assume that these incidents only occurred during biblical times. Further explorations reveal that, in early Rome, fathers had the power to kill, abandon, or sell their children (Thomas, 1972). The notion that a child must be worthy of survival was common throughout cultures.

Plato and Aristotle argued that children with physical or mental handicaps would only weaken the species and therefore urged that parents kill their defective children (Wallace, 1999). If a child cannot positively contribute to society, then that child should not be a member of society.

In the seventeenth and eighteenth centuries, in countries such as Germany or in the Native American cultures, infants were thrown into rivers or pools of water to determine their strength or worthiness; infants who did not surface were not rescued from drowning (Martin, 1972; Damme, 1978). A child who drowned was a weak child. In addition, for an infant to live, he/she must be acknowledged by the father (Radbill, 1987). If the father did not identify the child as his then the child would be killed or left to die. The bodies of children have been found buried in the foundations of buildings and structures such as the London Bridge (Sorel, 1984). Today, on almost a daily basis, the remains of children are found in landfills and in trash containers (Crosson-Tower, 1999). Therefore, the killing of children or infanticide (if the murder is of a child under the age of 1 year) has been demonstrated to exist not only today but throughout history. Add to that the fact that children are often not killed but beaten or sexually assaulted by adults provides one with a grim view of human beings and our willingness to care for our young.

It was quite common in the Middle Ages for children to be "rented" to other adults by their parents as indentured servants for years of service (some up until age 24) (Crosson-Tower, 1999). These child servants were at the mercy of their masters, much like the African American slaves during the nineteenth century, with their physical and emotional care totally under the control of their masters. In many instances, these indentured servants were sexually abused and/or physically abused (Sanger, 1898); however, just as is the case in the "traditional" parent-child relationship, much of the physical abuse was in the name of discipline.

Theologian John Calvin, a founder of modern Protestantism, supported the physical punishment (e.g., beatings) of children as he deemed it necessary to rid the child of evil and to produce an adult who would contribute in some positive manner to society. Only an obedient child could produce a productive adult citizen (Chesser, 1952). By physically punishing him or her, the child's will is broken, and the child may then be molded into a worthy adult (Crosson-Tower, 1999).

As the Industrial Revolution began, much of the hard labor was performed by the hands of children; thus, another aspect of child abuse in the form of child labor was established. Children, who were naturally smaller than adults, were ideal for jobs such as cleaning a printing press or sweeping a chimney (Stadum, 1995). In addition, child labor was cheap and, in the event of a fatal accident, a child was disposable (Stadum, 1995). It was not until the Child Labor Laws in the late 1800s that children began to be viewed as more than just laborers. Up until then there was no concept of a child being an individual in need of protection (especially not protection from a loved one); thus, there were not any legal support systems to ensure the rights of children. Simply stated, children had no rights. This changed with a young girl named Mary Ellen Wilson.

Mary Ellen Wilson was an 8-year-old girl in New York City in 1874. She was beaten and starved by her parents on a regular basis. This abuse continued, and there were no legal means of protection for Mary Ellen (Riis, 1892). At most, law enforcement officers could require that noise levels be minimized. When legal authorities finally intervened, they did so under the umbrella of the Prevention of Cruelty to Animals Act. The fact that animals were worthy of protection while children were not indicated a higher value on, say, a horse than a daughter. To those involved in the legal system and the supporters of children's rights, this seemed absurd.

Afterwards, the rights of legal intervention were extended in an attempt to protect these children under the Prevention of Cruelty to Children Act in 1875. This Act, in theory, protected children from physical abuse and neglect.

Unfortunately, there was little effort by the criminal justice community to aggressively address the physical abuse of children. However, if a case was reported to law enforcement officials, it was, by law, provided an avenue of investigation. The courts did little to prosecute offenders; the child was simply removed from the abusive home and placed in a supposedly non-abusive environment. Criminal justice officials made few efforts to monitor the well-being of the child. In fact, some researchers suggest that even today (especially in rural areas) a child's death is less likely to be investigated than an adult's (Unnithan, 1994). In a case of child sexual abuse, for the most part and from a criminal justice perspective, the topic was taboo.

Again, the Bible contains descriptions of the sexual abuse, incest, and rape of children. Specifically, in the Old Testament, Lot offered his daughters as sexual sacrifices in order to protect his visitor Abraham. In Greek mythology, Hercules raped the daughters of Theseus. In turn, legend has it that Theseus raped Helen of Troy when she was around the age of 7. Prior to the nineteenth century, it has been suggested that child marriages for girls were prevalent, and often, if the young girl was not married prior to menstruation, her family was disgraced (Wallace, 1999). In fact, betrothals of young girls (some under the age of 12) were sealed (with their fathers' permission) with intercourse (Crosson-Tower, 1999), and incest, just as today, was present in the homes (Morgan, 1877; Malinowski, 1927). In French medieval literature there are instances of men loaning their wives and/or daughters to male houseguests to make them feel welcome. The females of the family were the property of the male head of the household, and, as property, their owner decided their destiny. During the Victorian Era, child prostitutes were viewed as a necessary evil as they satisfied a husband's desire for sex without burdening the wife (Crosson-Tower, 1999). Finally, during the period of African American slavery in the United States, women would often be impregnated by their white masters to produce more slaves or used to sexually satisfy the white men.

Today, the expectations and value of female virginity vary by country. In the United States, many young women participate in sexual relations prior to legal adulthood. In India, virgin females are covenanted; thus, it is suggested that males are the victims of sexual abuse (Crosson-Tower, 1999). With the introduction of the Internet, incidents of child pornography and of adults meeting children through the Internet and later engaging them in sexual activities have increased (McCabe, 2000). However, there is little remedy for this with the exception of the criminal justice system's reactive efforts to report, investigate, and prosecute those individuals who abuse children.

Purpose of This Book

The purpose of this text is to provide readers with a basic foundation on the topic of child abuse. Readers will be able to: (1) identify and define the various categories of child abuse; (2) identify and discuss current statistics on child abuse; (3) identify and discuss theories that attempt to explain child abuse; and (4) identify and discuss criminal justice efforts to prevent child abuse; and (5) identify and discuss the community's primary and secondary abuse prevention efforts as well as sources for further information on the topic of child abuse.

This text is organized to provide straightforward information on each category of abuse: Chapter 2—Physical Abuse; Chapter 3—Sexual Abuse; Chapter 4—Emotional Abuse; Chapter 5—Neglect; and Chapter 6—Protecting the Child. At the end of chapters 2 through 5 are questions formulated from the materials presented within the chapter. Finally, the Appendices contain national sources for information on child abuse in addition to a suggested reading list of mass-market books on child abuse. This text not only provides information on child abuse but provides its readers with a baseline of information for the protection of children.

CHAPTER 2

Physical Abuse

On November 4, 1987, with the death of New York's 6-year-old Lisa Steinberg at the hands of her adoptive father, Joel Steinberg, who acknowledged "disciplining" his daughter while his girlfriend, Hedda Nussbaum, stood by, child physical abuse again appeared on the front page of America's society. The media and the criminal justice system were moved to action; however, one wonders what role (if any) criminal justice responses play in the picture of child abuse; does their presence stop child abuse? Or does their presence simply displace the violence?

On December 8, 2001, in New Orleans a mother's boyfriend was charged with shaking her 14-month-old son so violently that he died (Stanley, 2001). Eleven days later, on December 19, 2001, in New York, another child was killed by another boyfriend as the mother stood by (Kelley, 2001). Despite efforts to educate the American public about the physical vulnerabilities of small children, one must wonder, are these efforts in vain?

Throughout history, society has viewed the physical abuse of children as either a family problem or a child welfare problem, and aggressive efforts to reduce child abuse by the law enforcement community were not truly made until the late 1960s. However, today most citizens are aware that assaulting a child is a crime (Finkelhor & Ormrod, 2001; Barkan, 2001) just as assaulting an adult is a crime. Whether it is the medical community that defines physical abuse as related to ailments, symptoms, and injuries or the legal community that sees abuse in terms of intent, the abuse of children has become a concern for everyone (Crosson-Tower, 1999). No longer are most individuals willing to stand by when a child faces physical injury. No longer is law enforcement "powerless" in protecting children from family members. No longer is a child's report of abuse ignored.

This chapter summarizes the physical and behavioral indicators of child physical abuse, examines the abusers themselves, and provides some theoretical explanations of physical abuse. Also addressed in this chapter are ritualistic abuse, parental responses to physical abuse, and the most severe outcome of physical abuse—death. Finally, this chapter discusses recent reactions to child physical abuse from the criminal justice system (law enforcement personnel, prosecutors, and courts).

> Child physical abuse is the non-accidental injury of a child or children inflicted by a person (Crosson-Tower, 1999).

In 1994, the National Center on Child Abuse and Neglect (NCCAN), surveyed 50 states, the District of Columbia, the Virgin Islands, and all branches of the U.S. military to determine the incidence of child physical abuse. From those reporting jurisdictions, there were over 600,000 substantiated cases of physical abuse in the four-month period of September through December 1993—essentially, 150,000 cases per month (Sedlak & Broadhurst, 1996).

Another report, which utilized the National Incident-Based Reporting System (NIBRS) and was produced by the Federal Bureau of Investigation (FBI), suggested that the majority of child victims of physical abuse/assault were between the ages of 12–17 (61%) with approximately 11% under the age of 4 (FBI, 1997). Many researchers in the area of child victimization also suggest that some children are inherently at a higher risk for abuse than other children (Ounsted, Oppenheimer, & Lindsay, 1974). These "at-risk" children include healthy infants born from an unplanned pregnancy or a difficult pregnancy and/or delivery, children born with physical handicaps and/or mental handicaps, fussy and hyperactive children, or those children who cry excessively. In these cases, the children are more likely to be victims of child physical abuse.

Fortunately for child victims, in most cases of physical abuse, there are clear signs or signals of the abuse on the child's body. In fact, for the law enforcement officer, physical abuse is perhaps one of the easiest forms of child abuse to document and investigate. However, some cases of physical abuse are revealed only in terms of behavioral signs or indicators. The following sections discuss the physical and behavioral indicators of child physical abuse.

Physical Indicators

Just as physical evidence often remains at a crime scene, physical evidence (or a physical indicator) is often present in a case of physical abuse. The physical indicators of child abuse may include bruises, burns, fractures, head and/or internal injuries, lacerations, loss of teeth, gunshot injuries, and other unusual injuries such as human bite marks and bald spots. With these indicators, a report of physical abuse may be substantiated. The most appropriate person(s) to examine a child for indicators of physical abuse is a physician or a healthcare professional. When investigating cases of physical abuse, an investigator must consider the fact that childhood injuries do occur without intent and, therefore, must always be concerned with protecting not only the children but also the parents or caretakers in those cases that are *not* child abuse. Again, for most individuals defining child physical abuse in the legal community, *intent* is a key element.

Bruises

For this discussion, a *bruise* is defined as an injury that causes a bleeding of capillaries under the skin as a result of some external force placed upon the skin of the child.

All children acquire bruises; however, the color, the shape, and the location of the bruise on a child (especially a child under the age of 1 year) is an indicator of possible physical abuse (McNeese & Hebeler, 1977). Specifically, just as we have all viewed bruises that are black, purple, or yellow, the color of the bruise in many ways provides information on the injury. A bruise on a light-skinned individual, assuming a normal nutritional state of the child, which is blue is usually between 6 and 12 hours old (Davis, 1982). A bruise that is black or purple is usually about 12 to 24 hours old, and one that is pale green or yellow is usually over 5 days old (Davis, 1982). Of course, on darker skin, a bruise may be harder to detect. However, a child who has multiple bruises of varying shades of color, hence a child with bruises that have occurred at different times, may be a victim of physical abuse. A child who falls once will not have bruises of various colors but should have bruises of similar color and the bruises should be only on places that were contact points in the fall.

In regard to the location of a bruise or bruises, it is expected that children, especially toddlers, will get bruises on the fronts of their legs, their elbows, and other parts of the body that come in contact with the ground in a fall; however, bruises in other locations such as the back of the legs, the ears, the neck, and the forearms and/or upper arms may be indicators of abuse. A child who falls, just as is the case with an adult who falls, will attempt to catch himself with his/her hands or knees; therefore, bruises on the thighs or on areas not used in defensive postures are cause for concern. Specifically, bruises on the backs of the legs may indicate that a child has been hit from behind; a bruise on the earlobe may indicate that the child has been grabbed by the ear; a bruise on the neck may indicate an attempt at strangulation, and a bruise on the upper arm or forearm may indicate that a child has been grabbed or even held against his/her will (Crosson-Tower, 1999).

In considering the shape of a bruise, the weapon (whether it be a human hand or another weapon) used to produce the bruise will often reveal itself on the skin of the child victim. Bruises, in most cases, will be in the shape of a hand or of the fingers of the hand, a fist, or some sort of a paddle that immediately reveals to the examiner the mode of injury. Bruises that occur in a linear pattern often indicate the use of a belt, whip, or an old-fashioned "switch" (a small tree branch). Bruises in the pattern of a small circle may indicate a ring pattern and abuse by fists. Bruises that are oval-shaped such as in a loop formation may indicate the use of a cord such an extension cord or an iron cord. Again, multiple bruises of varying shapes, colors, and locations are prime indicators of a pattern of physical abuse and should "red flag" immediate concern and action to ensure the victim's safety.

Burns

Burns are defined in terms of first degree, second degree, and third degree, depending on how many layers of skin are burned with a first degree burn the least serious. Burns to children are generally caused by heat or friction. Infections to the untreated burned areas are also a concern.

Burns can result in permanent injury or death of the child (Pressel, 2000). Burns may be in the shape of irons, curling irons, or range-top burners. Burns that leave centimeter-long circular marks may indicate cigarette burns (Pressel, 2000), and those a bit larger but still round may indicate a cigarette lighter such as one found in a vehicle. Scald marks on the hands, feet, or buttocks that have a glove or mitten appearance usually indicates a deliberate immersion of the child in hot water. Additionally, splash burns or burns on areas not usually exposed in accidental spills may also suggest physical abuse. However, in the case of burns, one must also consider the family background as many cultures and/or religions may practice the burning of certain areas of the body either as a ritual (as will be discussed later in this chapter) or a component of folk medicine. It would be unfortunate and would place the accusing agency in a vulnerable position for a lawsuit to accuse a parent of physical abuse when the burn was inflicted in an attempt to "heal" the child. However, as law enforcement would probably maintain, regardless of the philosophy behind the burning, an intentional burn is child abuse.

Fractures

In this discussion, a fracture is defined as a broken bone. A fracture is treated by aligning the broken bone to allow it to regenerate or heal. The presence of fractures, especially in infants, may be a sign of physical abuse (Crosson-Tower, 1999). When investigating fractures, one must review both the location and extent of the injury. The abused child may be subjected to multiple fractures at one time or single fractures over time, spiral fractures, greenstick fractures, subperiosteal fractures, and dislocations (Crosson-Tower, 1999).

Children break bones often in accidents; however, fractures are also very common in cases of physical abuse. In cases where there is a history of child abuse, multiple fractures, all done at different times, may be present.

One type of fracture, the *spiral fracture,* is very common in child abuse. In this type of injury, the abuser most often causes the fracture to the bone by using a twisting motion or a sudden jerk on the child's arm or leg. It is extremely rare for spiral fractures to occur in children under the age of 3 as their bones are much more limber than those of older children or adults (Wallace, 1999); it is nearly impossible for this sort of injury to indicate anything other than abuse.

Another type of fracture that may occur in a case of physical abuse is a *greenstick fracture*. In this type of fracture, one side of the bone is broken while the other side is bent (Faller and Ziefert, 1981). This type of injury might occur if a child were struck suddenly and with great force on one side of a bone located in an area such as the lower leg. This type of fracture is common in accidents but also often present in the cases of abuse.

In a *subperiosteal fracture* the bone is broken but without a resulting change in its contour and may heal with only calcium deposits remaining around the break as signs of a previous injury (Faller & Ziefert, 1981). With subperiosteal fractures, the injury is usually discovered by accident or by a physician attempting to establish a pattern of physical abuse.

Finally, a *dislocation* is a fracture in which the bone is separated from its joint. Dislocations may occur by accident or in a case of abuse, especially in cases in which the abuser suddenly grabbed the child by the arm while the child was attempting to flee (Faller & Ziefert, 1981). Investigators examining fractures for evidence of abuse must carefully consider the explanation of the incident before declaring child abuse.

Head/Internal Injuries

In head or internal injuries, there are many possible outcomes resulting from abuse. Although head injuries occur in all children, infants because of their physical state, are especially vulnerable to this result of child abuse. In infants, injuries to the top of the head, which would not have occurred in a "typical" fall, may indicate abuse. Whiplash and neurological damage that result in *Shaken Baby Syndrome* also occur with infants and are in most cases undetectable except by a physician. Shaken Baby Syndrome, an accepted medical diagnosis, is caused when a child's head is whipped back and forth or from side to side as the abuser shakes the baby (Wallace, 1999). This whipping motion, which causes the brain to move within the skull, may cause retinal damage, and hemorrhaging in the brain and can lead to permanent brain damage or death (Wallace, 1999). Shaken Baby Syndrome may occur when a parent becomes impatient and hostile toward a child who is crying and shakes the child in an attempt to frighten him/her into silence.

Abused children may also experience other internal injuries such as a ruptured spleen or liver, a kidney or bladder injury, or an injury to the pancreas such as would occur in the event of applied force such as a fist to that area of the body. Abused children may also experience damage to internal organs from intentional dehydration and poisoning. Unfortunately, for these most severe types of injuries, only trained medical professionals can detect the abuse. Also, in cases of these most severe types of injuries, only medical professionals can prevent these abuses from resulting in death.

Other Injuries

Although bruises, burns, and fractures are probably the most common signs of physical abuse, other types of injuries signal child abuse. For example, lacerations, cuts and stab wounds, human bites, or loss of teeth, bald spots on the head, and firearms injuries. Cuts, stabs, and human bites are prime indicators of not only physical abuse but a propensity of some individual toward extreme violence. In cases such as these, the child is at high risk for not only permanent injury but death.

As with the other more common injuries, there are three elements to consider when alleging child abuse. Those elements are the location of the injury, the history of the injury, and the treatment of that injury. For example, the location of a cut may provide information on its cause. It is expected that during normal daily play, children will obtain cuts and scratches on their knees, elbows, and hands; however, cuts or lacerations on the palms of their hands, or the undersides of their forearms may be defensive cuts and may have been acquired in a hands and arms over the face position to prevent injury to the face. Today, as many child abusers are now aware of the consequences of being identified as an abuser, lacerations to the bottom of the feet and other areas of the body normally covered by clothing during the school day are not uncommon.

A child who has on his or her body multiple cuts, especially those cuts that differ in age and healing, may be a child with a history of physical abuse, and just as it is not unusual for adult victims of physical abuse to not receive medical treatment after every incident of abuse, the same is true for child victims. An untreated laceration will in most cases leave a larger scar than those that were treated. A child with a history of untreated lacerations may be a victim of physical abuse.

Determining a case of physical abuse, which is probably the easiest form of abuse to determine for medical and criminal justice practicioners, is not a simple task. Children, at many times over their young lives, may experience injuries consistent with physical abuse. Therefore, before the assertion of physical abuse is made, a good investigator considers the child's and the caretaker's explanations (if there are any explanations) for the injury. In the case of an injury with conflicting explanations, an evaluation must be completed by the investigator before alleging child abuse.

Behavioral Indicators

In some cases of physical abuse, the physical injuries go undetected; in those cases, the behavioral symptoms or indicators are the most visible clues of abuse. The behavioral indicators of child physical abuse may be different in each child; however, there are certain common behaviors seen more often in children with a history of physical abuse than in children without such a history. Those symptoms vary to include extreme individual behaviors such as aggressiveness or withdrawn personalities, poor social relations with peers and adults, learning problems such as delayed language development or poor academic performance, and delinquency (Wallace, 1999). Although these symptoms do not always indicate abuse, children who display two or

more of these behavioral indicators may be victims of physical abuse and should be identified.

The image of the abused child who is easily frightened by
adults is not simply a made-for-the movies character. Often
in cases of physical abuse, children are afraid of not only
their parents but also other authority figures such as teachers or other adults. These children may exhibit a fear of
adult presence, a fear of failure in the presence of adults
(Rodeheffer and Martin, 1976), and/or a fear of returning to
their homes (Wallace, 1999). In addition, these children
with very low self-esteem may appear hostile or indifferent
or lack the capacity to enjoy life (Martin and Beezley, 1976).
Additionally, it is not uncommon for a victim of patterned
physical abuse to regress into acting as if he/she is still an infant with "baby talk" and "accidents" such as wetting his/
her pants. The abused children, not positively reinforced in
their age-appropriate behaviors may seem displaced in
terms of their age and their actions.

Infants who are physically abused and, of course, unable
to verbally report the abuse may behave differently from infants who have not been physically abused. Physically
abused infants may exhibit a passive watchfulness with little
expectation of parental comfort (Martin, 1972). These children do not seek comfort from their parents or caretakers
and exhibit little expectation of comfort from other persons.
Children ages 5–9, and in some cases toddlers, may appear
pseudo-mature or old for their years with an almost compul-
sive concern for order and details (Martin and Beezley, 1976).
These children, in many cases, provide the necessities of
food and comfort for themselves and perhaps even for their
younger siblings. In addition, it would not be unusual for a
physically abused child to wear clothing that is clearly intended to cover the body when not seasonally appropriate
such as a long-sleeved shirt on an 85° day (Wallace, 1999).

Social Behaviors and Learning Problems

Children who have been victims of physical abuse, because
they have not experienced positive role models, often lack

the capacity to form appropriate social relationships (Crosson-Tower, 1999). Specifically, in relationships with adults and other children, the children who have been victims of physical abuse often have unstable relationships with behavior ranging from extremely violent interactions to no interactions at all. Also, the language development of abused children may be inhibited since often their attempts at verbalization were met with physical abuse (Rodeheffer & Martin, 1976); therefore, the everyday conversations that most individuals take for granted are not always possible for the abused child.

In addition, as language development is delayed for many abused children, learning problems in the classroom are apparent. A child who has been a victim of physical abuse in the home may often also suffer the consequences of an uninvolved parent in the school setting. Because of this lack of support, it is not uncommon for abused children to perform poorly in school either because of the pain of physical beatings the night before, the fear of authority figures, or hostility toward others in their environment. With little attention to academics at home, children who are victims of physical abuse rarely shine in the school setting, and it is unrealistic, in most cases, to expect outstanding academic performances from children who focus most of their efforts on avoiding victimization.

Delinquency and Criminal Behavior

Finally, one other area of both short-term and long-term consequences of child abuse is delinquency and criminal behavior. A vast amount of literature exists on the relationship of conditions of home life, physical abuse, and the propensity toward juvenile delinquency. As supported by the notion of a "Cycle of Violence" (described later in this chapter), a child who has been raised in a violent environment is more likely to become violent (Bynum & Thompson, 2002). Many males will grow up to be the abusers; females, on the other hand, in most cases, will continue to be victims. In addition, children who are victims of physical abuse are more likely to become runaways, exhibit disruptive and/or truant behaviors in school, use drugs and alcohol, and become involved in deviant sexual behaviors (Bartollas, 2000). Many of these deviant and/or criminal behaviors result in premature death for the child victim.

Child Abusers

The physical abusers of a child are those most likely to be in the presence of that child. In particular, the physical abusers of children are, in the majority of the cases, the parents, caretakers, and/ or siblings of the children.

Parents and Caretakers

Personality Traits. Many researchers and authorities of child abuse assert that parents and caretakers who physically abuse their children, demonstrate similar personality characteristics (Crosson-Tower, 1999). The first of those traits is low self-esteem. These parents, for whatever reason, see themselves as inadequate and are in an almost continuous search for the recognition, respect, and acceptance of others. Children, with their developing needs for exploration and questions, pose a threat to these individuals in terms of controllability, the testing of limits, and their constant inquiries of "Why?" A parent who fears exposure of either a physical or behavioral flaw may lash out at the child in an attempt of control or to disguise those personal vulnerabilities.

A second common personality trait of physically abusive parents or caretakers is emotional immaturity. Many parents are immature in terms of expectations, their understanding of a child's capacity for responsibilities, and the amount and kind of gratification they expected from those children. If the immature parent has unrealistic expectations of the child and the child fails to meet that expectation, the parent may respond with violence. This "violent nature" of the parents or advanced stages of anger mismanagement is significant in predicting a child's risk of physical abuse (Jackson, Thompson, Christiansen, Colman, Wyatt, Buckendahl, Wilcox & Peterson, 1999). One stage of childhood development cited again and again as making the child especially vulnerable to physical abuse is the stage of potty or toilet training. In particular, although parents may be aware that toilet training is a process of learning, they may become impatient and, in the event of an "accident," violent with the child.

Finally, it is not unusual for parents and/or caretakers who physically abuse their children to have problems with addiction or drug abuse. Alcohol is the most common drug. Alcoholic parents, because of their impairments from the alcohol, are more likely to physically abuse their children. The children of alcoholic parents, in many cases, satisfy their own basic needs without the assistance of their parents; however, the alcoholic parent, who may also possess unrealistic expectations of childhood and the household responsibilities of the child, may react with violence to the child who fails to satisfy the parent's expectation.

Other explanations for child physical abuse by parents or caretakers include the concept of punishment. Many abusers of children, in terms of physical abuse, do so in the name of discipline. This "discipline" is often a learned behavior, the manner in which the abuser's parents controlled his/her behavior; therefore, it seems like a normal role of parenting. Many researchers conclude that abusers fail to clearly differentiate between punishment or corporal punishment and child abuse.

Environmental Stresses. Finally, the environmental stresses that surround the home are also cited as reasons for the physical abuse of children. Marital problems such as infidelity or domestic violence as well as unemployment and financial problems further aggravate an already-sensitive home and may increase the likelihood of child physical abuse. In particular, isolation or a lack of family social support is also identified as a risk factor for abuse. Parents who have no one else to assist in the everyday activities of raising children often become irritated by their children and are, in many cases, likely to physically lash out at them.

Munchausen Syndrome by Proxy. An increasing number of law enforcement and social service agencies are becoming aware of a special type of child physical abuse called Munchausen Syndrome by Proxy (Crosson-Tower, 1999). This syndrome, which affects, in most cases, mothers and their infants or young children, involves a mother who seeks medical attention on a regular basis for her sick child. Unfortunately, the mother actually causes the child's illness (Stone, 1989). These mothers or caretakers will seek the immediate attention of hospital employees while portraying themselves as the dedicated and loving mother of a very sick child. At the same time, the mother may be administering doses of substances such as Ipecac to produce vomiting or phenolphthalein to cause diarrhea in an attempt to create and maintain that sick child. The mother, who has been identified as the mother of an extremely ill child, receives attention and sympathy from the hospital staff, family, and friends while her child endures the painful medical tests to determine the cause of the illness. This abuse of children by the mother may be exhibited in patterns of behavior that may include multiple children within the family. Unfortunately, in some cases of Munchausen Syndrome by Proxy, children eventually die.

Siblings

One source of physical abuse, often overlooked in the investigations of such cases, are siblings of the abused child. Many researchers are now recognizing abuse by siblings and profiling would-be abusers to reduce the incidence of sibling abuse. Physical abuse by siblings may be divided into three forms: (1) common (2) unusual, and (3) injurious (Wiehe, 1997). In the common form of physical abuse, siblings hit, bite, and shove each other. In these cases of abuse, the abusing sibling is usually much larger and stronger than the victim. Thus, the child cannot defend himself/herself from the abusive older brother or sister. Sibling jealousy is often the motivating factor behind this type of abuse; however, as we know, not all jealous siblings abuse each other. The un- usual form of physical abuse includes such actions as tick- ling and/or restraining the victim. Although not thought to cause permanent damage to the child, victims of tickling may report later in life that they still feel controlled by oth- ers and dislike any sort of touching by other human beings (Wiehe, 1997). We have all experienced tickling from some other person as a form of play; however, tickling a child to a point of pain or helplessness is abuse. In addition, restrain- ing an individual not only may cause a feeling of powerless- ness but also, in some states, is considered kidnapping (a criminal offense). Finally, injurious abuse includes actions such as smothering, holding someone's head underwater, choking, and shooting a child with a BB or pellet gun (Wiehe, 1997). Again, although historically thought to result in only physical pain or abuse, victims of injurious sibling abuse may be left with not only the physical injury from the abuse but also such lasting effects such as fear of water or small places or the feeling that they are still accessible to the abusers—thus, still vulnerable for victimization.

Sibling abusers often exhibit the same personality char- acteristics as adult abusers. These children, in an attempt to maintain control over their, in most cases, younger siblings resort to physically abusing them. Over time, the physical abuse at the hands of siblings, as well as with adult abusers, may increase in frequency and severity. The long-term ef- fects may be permanent physical injury or emotional injury and even death. The victimization usually continues until the parents intervene or the victim discovers a way to end it. Some victims finally confront their abusive siblings, and some victims end their abuse by simply moving away from their abusers.

Abuse Theories

There are a variety of theoretical explanations for the physical abuse of children that include both internal and external factors. Four such explanations are included in this text: (1) the Cycle of Violence; (2) the Psychodynamic Model; (3) the Environmental Stress Model, and (4) Victim Precipitation. The chapter also covers the concept of ritualistic abuse, an increasingly common explanation for physical abuse.

The Cycle of Violence

The Intergenerational Transmission of Violence Theory or the *Cycle of Violence* as it is commonly known, maintains that violence, which includes the physical abuse of children, is a learned behavior within the family system that is passed from parent to child and generation to generation (Wallace, 1999). A number of views may explain how child physical abuse may be passed from generation to generation.

One theory is that in domestic situations of violence, children learn the parent role through observation; those who grow up in an abusive situation believe that harsh parenting and physical punishment are normal (Siegel, 2000). Harsh parenting teaches children hitting is necessary to maintain control; a child who is hit is also likely to hit (Simon, Wu, Johnson & Conger, 1995).

Physical violence either experienced or witnessed by the child, is continued when the child becomes a parent. This theory suggests that today's child victims of violence at home will be tomorrow's adult abusers of their children (Wallace, 1999). This theory also suggests that only through intervention will the cycle of abuse be broken, and, since in most cases intervention does not occur, the abuse continues.

The Psychodynamic Model

The *Psychodynamic Model,* also called the Psychopathological Model (Gelles, 1973), maintains that the personality of the parents, in particular, the lack of bonding in the relationship between parent and child, is a key factor in the abuse of children (Aber & Allen, 1987; Ainsworth, Blehar, Waters & Wall, 1978). In cases of abuse such as these, the parent, because of his/her inability to trust, emotional immaturity, or lack of involvement with the child, will fail to form a bond with that child. This lack of a nurturing bond, in combination with a child of a different temperament than the parent's or a specific conflict, increases the likelihood of physical violence. The child, because of his/her smaller stature, becomes the victim; the parent is the abuser.

Another aspect of this model is role reversal. In many cases, parents or caretakers who are unable to see themselves in a parenting role will expect the child to assume the role of the nurturer and to initiate the bonding process (Crosson-Tower, 1999). When the child fails to initiate the bonding or does not provide the parents with the love and attention they expect, the parents may react with physical abuse. It is also asserted that parents who physically abuse their children do so because of their inability to understand appropriate child and adult behaviors (Milner & Dopke, 1997).

The Environmental Stress Model

The *Environmental Stress Model* suggests that stress in the environment is the key cause of abuse. Many researchers have suggested that the more stressful the environment, the more likely the event of physical abuse (Gil, 1970). Specifically, stresses such as unemployment, poor education, poverty, racism, and sexism increase the risk of child physical abuse (Crosson-Tower, 1999). Parents who experience these stresses are more likely to be unhappy in their roles as parents and thus are more likely to abuse their children. Embedded in the concept of the Environmental Stress Model is *Strain Theory*. Criminologists who view crime as related to lower-class frustration and anger are referred to as Strain theorists (Siegel, 2000). Strain Theory, the desire for success coupled with the lack of opportunity produces strain and frustration (Siegel, 2000). Parents, who are unable to achieve the goals that they have set for themselves become violent. Rather than striking the employer who has failed to provide him/her with a raise, the parent strikes his/her child. Children, again, because of their smaller size and inability to fight back, become the victims of physical abuse.

Victim Precipitation

In the hypothesis of *Victim Precipitation,* victimization is a result of some action or behavior by the victim. The major premise is that the victim provokes the criminal acts by some action (Siegel, 2000). This model of victim-precipitated victimization was first studied in the late 1950s by Marvin Wolfgang as he applied the concept to criminal homicides (Wolfgang, 1958). Today the concept is often applied to the crime of "simple rape" or date rape.

In regard to the physical abuse of children, some children may, because of their personality or disposition, fail to support the opinions of a parent and, in fact, very aggressively verbalize their disagreement. To some parents who are unskilled in non-physical forms of discipline, a child who fails to conform or act as a parent has envisioned and then perhaps argues with the parent over the action initiates the attack (in the eyes of the parent). Simply stated, the child, because he/she does not satisfy the parent's expectation of appropriate behavior, is then beaten—physically abused.

Ritualistic Abuse

Finally, one type of physical abuse that is often overlooked or discounted in the literature is ritualistic abuse. Although the definition of ritualistic abuse is still evolving (Wallace, 1999), it is based on the philosophy that physical abuse is rarely a single incident and that physical abuse can manifest itself in many different forms, cutting or branding of the child being two of the most common examples. However, it must be acknowledged that some ritualistic actions of abuse are based upon cultural or religious ideas and are enacted to ensure the well-being of the child.

Through ritualistic physical abuse, the cult (or the care-takers) reinforces its "ownership" of the child victim. The child's abuse leaves a permanent injury or mark on the child; thus, the child is identified by his/her mark. In the 1980s, across the nation, the media devoted a tremendous amount of attention to reports of satanic ritualistic child abuse when, in fact, the confirmed cases were few and far between (Bottoms & Davis, 1997). However, parents, who feared for the safety of their children and the victimization of their child at the hands of a stranger, insisted upon concentrated efforts by law enforcement agencies to seek and destroy cults that worshipped the devil. At that time, and as is supported historically, children were not the victims of mass destruction through ritualistic abuse but rather victimized by their own parents without the influence of Satan or another supreme being.

Cases encountered by clinical psychologists within the United States indicate that only a very small minority of the psychologists had ever encountered cases of ritualistic child abuse (Bottoms, Shaver & Goodman, 1996). Thus, ritualistic abuse, of concern for many citizens interested in preventing child abuse, was essentially not something to worry about.

Parental Responses

Most often in the case of child physical abuse, the abuser is a parent; therefore, parental responses are minimal. In most cases, the parent justifies the abuse in the name of discipline and punishment. The parent places the blame for the abuse on the child because the child's behavior warranted the punishment. In the case of severe abuse, some parents may feel remorse, and, in an attempt to remedy the situation, the parent and child may enter into a "honeymoon stage" similar to the loving stage that often follows an incident of adult domestic violence.

In the cases of child physical abuse where the abuser is a

sibling, parental responses vary. In some instances, a parent will address the situation and the abuse will end; however, that is not always the case. Often in cases of sibling abuse, parents ignore or minimize the incident by rationalizing the problem as sibling rivalry, blaming the victim for instigating the violence, or by reacting with indifference to the situation (Weihe, 1997). If the parents do not intervene, the abuse will most likely continue until the victim ends the abuse.

Death

Unfortunately, some cases of child physical abuse end in death. The child, because of his/her small physical statue is especially vulnerable to physical abuse. Especially in the case of infants, Shaken Baby Syndrome and Munchausen by Proxy may result in death of the child. As violence escalates in abuse situations, children often become homicide victims. Today, the death of children through physical abuse is being considered by many to be a national epidemic. Increasingly, when a child dies as a result of abuse, the specific cause of death is identified, and the parents and/or caretakers are prosecuted in criminal court (Crosson-Tower, 1999).

Criminal Justice Responses

Recently, in the criminal justice system, the phenomenon of child physical abuse has received most attention in conjunction with domestic violence and mandatory arrest policies of local law enforcement agencies. Under the policy of mandatory arrest, if evidence exists of physical violence against an individual, then the accused abuser is arrested; however, in the case of child physical abuse (under the notion of domestic authority) the law recognizes the right of parents to physically discipline their children in a reasonable manner (Reid, 1995). In addition, *in loco parentis* (in the place of parents), teachers and guardians also have the right to physically discipline (use corporal punishment) their children as the Supreme Court has ruled that school children may be paddled (Reid, 1995).

In cases of child physical abuse, law enforcement officials are often left to determine if the child was "spanked" or abused. For that determination, as stated earlier, they often base their decision upon location, extent, and history of injuries. Once the law enforcement officer decides to arrest those individuals believed to be responsible, most law enforcement agencies forward those arrested (or cleared) cases to their prosecutors for assessments on the cases in terms of legal matters (Neubauer, 1991). Just as with any criminal court case, child abuse cases begin with a formal filing of charges. The prosecutor now determines, based upon law enforcement's investigation, the law, and trend in conviction rates of child abuse cases, if charges of child physical abuse should be filed. In many cases, trends in conviction rates are the most difficult component to gauge.

Penal law as applied to the physical abuse of children includes murder, manslaughter, assault and battery, and statutory crimes of child maltreatment such as aggravated abuse and unreasonable corporal punishment (Goldstein, 1999). However, in many cases, prosecutors are aware of the fact that juries, in cases of child physical abuse, are often reluctant to convict abusers (especially parents) on charges of the most serious nature such as murder and that, in some cases, even if the jury finds an offender guilty of child physical abuse, those judgments may be reversed.

Specifically, in the case of the *State v. Thorpe (1981)*, a father charged with the murder of his 4-month-old daughter was convicted of only assault and battery (Goldstein, 1999). In the case of the *State of Ohio v. Higgins (1990)*, the conviction of a father found guilty of felonious assault and child endangering was overturned on the grounds of ineffective counsel, and in the case of the *State of North Carolina v. Byrd (1983)*, the Supreme Court reversed the conviction of guilty of involuntary manslaughter based upon the prosecutor's introduction of a history of abuse to other children in the family during closing arguments. Hence, in cases of child

PHYSICAL ABUSE

In November of 1987, 6-year-old Lisa Steinberg was beaten to death by her adoptive father Joel Steinberg. In 1989, Steinberg was found guilty of first-degree manslaughter and sentenced to 25 years in prison. In October of 1999, Lisa's biological mother, Michele Launders, who was appointed administrator of her daughter's estate, was awarded nearly $1million to settle her claim that city agencies such as the New York Department of Education, local police, and New York's Department of Social Services, failed to protect her daughter.

In this case, a history of responses by the police and the Department of Social Services to the home of Lisa Steinberg was documented to exist. During this suit it was also revealed that teachers and administrators who suspected abuse failed to report it.

physical abuse, prosecutors will often charge offenders with lesser offenses in order to gain a conviction or plea bargain a case to avoid trial.

In today's age of conflicting standards of child physical discipline and child abuse, it is understandable that common law grants parents the privilege to apply reasonable force to their child in order to control, train, or educate that child (Goldstein, 1999); however, the distinction between discipline and abuse is often unclear and one wonders what is "reasonable"? As reasonableness is a subjective standard, law enforcement personnel, and individuals in the criminal justice system are left without clarity of definition and are often times disappointed by a jury's decision of "not guilty" in cases of child physical abuse and, thus, in many cases, will choose to pursue only the most severe cases of child physical abuse—those that end in death. In those disappointing decisions of not guilty, the lost time and energy of those individuals is not only financial but also an emotional burden. In reality, more offenders are free to continue their abuse of children, and more children are at risk for victimization.

Conclusion

The physical abuse of children is a problem for not only the victim but also for society as a whole. Children who are victims of physical abuse not only suffer directly from their injuries but often also suffer indirectly in term of behavioral problems and long-term effects such as low self-esteem and the inability to form and maintain relationships with intimates as adults.

Despite recent efforts at the state and local level to reduce the incidents of physical abuse, the numbers continue to increase. Only through conscious efforts to reduce the actions do we expect physical abuse to end; only through conscious efforts do we expect children to be safe.

Questions

1. Child abuse is defined in terms of four categories of abuse. What is child physical abuse?
2. There are many indicators of child physical abuse. What are three of the physical indicators?
3. What are three of the behavioral indicators?
4. This chapter identified four theoretical explanations of physical abuse. What are the four explanations discussed in this chapter, and how do they explain child physical abuse?
5. What are some of the parental responses to physical abuse?

Questions for Discussion

1. Is there a difference between spanking a child and beating a child? Are the outcomes always distinguishable?
2. Is spanking ever necessary?
3. If you were a child, would a spanking or the fear of a spanking deter you from inappropriate behaviors?
4. As a prosecutor, are there advantages to pursuing cases of child physical abuse that may be perceived as "less severe"?
5. As a prosecutor, you have a choice between pursuing the gang-related murder case of a drive-by shooting or the murder case of child physical abuse. Which do you select? Why?

CHAPTER 3

SEXUAL ABUSE

Adam Walsh, Jacob Wetterling, Polly Klaas, and Megan Kanka have all helped to focus criminal justice efforts toward the prevention of child sexual abuse. Unfortunately, each of these children was either murdered and raped or assumed to be murdered by his or her assailants.

Adam Walsh, whose father hosted the television show *America's Most Wanted,* was a 6-year-old Florida boy who disappeared in 1981 while shopping with his mother. Only Adam's severed head was found—his body was never discovered.

In 1989, Jacob Wetterling was an 11-year-old boy from Minnesota who was abducted while riding his bike. Jacob has never been found. Although neither Adam nor Jacob were confirmed cases of sexual assault, most law enforcement officials and researchers in the area of child abductions assume the cases to be ones of molestation and murder.

In 1993, Polly Klaas was a 12-year-old California girl who was abducted from her home during a slumber party. Her abductor was convicted of her rape and murder.

Megan Kanka was a 7-year-old girl who, in 1994, was raped and murdered by a convicted sex offender who moved into her neighborhood after serving his sentence.

Sex with children has existed and been documented since biblical times. It is also an activity that is expected to continue. Of the four categories of child abuse, the last to receive public attention was child sexual abuse, mainly because most sexual abusers of children were family members, and, until recently, incest was not a topic for public conversation. Today sex with children or the sexual abuse of a child is a crime, and, for those in the criminal justice field as well as the general public, child sexual abuse is now a topic worthy of discussion and prevention.

> Child sexual abuse is the sexual exploitation or sexual activities with a child or children (Wallace, 1999). Child sexual abuse includes but is not limited to the fondling of a child's genitals, intercourse, incest, rape, sodomy, and the exploitation of children through the production and distribution of child pornography or child prostitution (ACF, 1999).

This chapter discusses the perpetrators of sexual abuse and profiles of child victims that include both physical and behavioral indicators of abuse. The chapter describes the progression, some theoretical explanations for this progression, the consequences to a child from a sexual assault, and the responses by the criminal justice system.

Based upon reports to police from 1986 to 1993, the estimated number of sexually abused children increased 83%, rising from 119,200 incidents to 217,700 incidents (Sedlak & Broadhurst, 1996). However, it must be acknowledged that many incidents of child sexual abuse remain unreported (FBI, 1997; Russell, 1983), and therefore, it is expected that child sexual abuse is even more prevalent than law enforcement reports establish. In fact, when comparing general rates of rape reported to law enforcement through the Uniform Crime Reports (UCR) and those reported on victimization surveys through the National Crime Victimization Survey (NCVS), it is estimated that only about one-third of the sex crimes that occur annually are reported to law enforcement (Barkan, 2001). Given the fact that infants and toddlers who are victims of sexual abuse may be unable to communicate their abuse leads many researchers to suggest that child sexual abuse is even more underreported than adult cases of sexual abuse. Despite that fact, current research on the prevalence of child sexual assaults indicates that incidents over the last few years have become significantly more severe and violent as a greater number of adult victims disclosed being raped as a child in the 1990s than in the 1980s; however, these incidents were not reported to police (Wyatt, Loeb, Solis, Carmona & Romero, 1999; Kercher & McShane, 1984). To address such a problem, one must first examine perpetrators of child sexual abuse.

Sources of Sexual Abuse

In research on the perpetrators of the sexual abuse of children, abuse is divided into two categories: familial and extrafamilial (abuse from someone outside of the family). However, in most cases of child sexual abuse, the perpetrator is a family member (Crosson-Tower, 2002; Clark, 1999; McCabe & Gregory, 1997) or a person living within the household. For example, on December 11th, 2001, in St. Louis, a man, residing in the home of friends, sexually assaulted their 9-year-old daughter (Schremp, 2001). On December 31st of the same year, a father in St. Louis was charged with sexually abusing two of his foster sons (Carroll, 2001). For ease in the dissemination of information on the sources of child sexual abuse in this text, a perpetrator is discussed relative to his/her relationship to the child.

Familial Abuse

The sexual abuse of a child by a family member is incest and, despite the taboo of incest, the activity remains a part of American households (Wyatt, Loeb, Solis, Carmona & Romero, 1999). According to Proximity Theory, victims do not encourage the activity, but rather they are in the wrong place at the wrong time. Often, in cases of incest, children are in the wrong place (their homes) at the wrong time.

The term incest most often refers to sexual relations between father and daughter; however, it also includes other family sexual relations such as between an uncle and child, a grandfather and grandchild, a mother and son, and siblings. Adults are generally assumed to be the perpetrators of incest; however, some researchers suggest that brother-sister sexual relationships are more common than father-daughter incest (Wiehe, 1997; Gebhard, Gagnon, Pomeroy & Christenson, 1965).

The literature suggests that incestuous families have similar characteristics (Crosson-Tower, 2002). They are often secretive in nearly all of their family activities, overly possessive of their children, and operate in an environment where the abused child and his/her abuser are often alone with each other (Sgroi, 1982).

Sexual abuse at the hands of a family member is, in many cases, more damaging in terms of long-term consequences than sexual abuse at the hands of a stranger (Gully, Britton, Hansen, Goodwin & Nope, 1999). Not only does the child suffer the physical and/or emotional damage of the incident(s) but also the damage related to a broken trust from an individual who is supposed to love and protect the child. Mayer (1983) suggests three categories of incest according to the degree of harm to the child. Those categories are: molestation, assault, and rape.

In *molestation* cases, the child is fondled and petted by the abuser, but intercourse between the child and abuser does not take place (Mayer, 1983). The child may not suffer physical signs such as vaginal tears or a bleeding rectum; however, the child may still be left with the emotional scars of abuse.

In *assault* intercourse may occur; however, the intercourse is usually not physically forced (Mayer, 1983). The child, under the influence of drugs or alcohol, may "consent" to having sex with the family member. In incestuous assaults, the child may be left with the physical signs of sexual abuse as well as the emotional scars of victimization.

Finally, in incestuous *rape,* the sexual assault is forced. The child has no control over the action and may also experience other types of abuse such as physical abuse and emotional abuse along with the sexual abuse. In these cases of incest, most researchers suggest that the child is most damaged both physically and emotionally. Specifically, the more violent the encounter, the more harm to the child (Crosson-Tower, 1999).

Father. In most cases of incest, the public assumes the father to be the perpetrator. No one clearly understands why one father can comfort his child in her bed after she has had a bad dream while another father upon entering the child's bedroom becomes sexually excited; however, the distinctions do exist and cases of father-child incest are common. Some researchers suggest that fathers will often distort the role of their child in order to rationalize the sexual encounter (Crosson-Tower, 1999). A father who, because of a wife's absence, sees his daughter as the homemaker and caretaker of his other children, may also view his daughter in a wife's role with the husband/wife "responsibilities" of sexual affection. There are also those researchers who suggest that incest is an avenue of control, and those fathers who engage in incest with their children do so in an attempt to maintain a position of power within the household. The child is the father's property, and as that property owner, the father has the right to use the child (his property), as he desires. The mother often remains ignorant of the activity, ignores the activity, or participates in the activity.

Mother. Although not the stereotypical family member to sexually abuse children, mothers are also perpetrators of abuse. In cases of mothers who sexually abuse their children, the physical evidence, such as sperm that may be present in father-perpetrated abuse, is not found. In addition, a mother may "mask" sexual abuse in the activities of bathing the child or changing the child's diaper. Few people would consider a mother who takes photos of her child in the bathtub to be an individual interested in distributing child pornography via the Internet.

Explanations for mother-inflicted sexual abuse include pedophilia (the physical attraction to young children) and profit in the prostitution of children or child pornography. A mother who is in need of money may market her sexual activities with her child. Finally, the mother who uses her child for a sexual partner may do so in attempt to maintain "closeness" in their relationship. These mothers, in many cases lacking an adult companion, make the child a substitute for an adult.

Combined Families. The combination of families provides another set of variables in the dynamics of incest. With these perpetrators the child's expectation of a father or mother role may be very real; however, the adult, without the bond that generally begins when the child comes home from the hospital, may view the child as simply another person— thus, the incest taboo is diminished. In today's society of "blended" families, incidents of this type of incest are expected to continue.

Sibling. There are those who feel that sibling incest is perhaps the most common form of incest. However, sexual relations between siblings are still incest. In many cases, incest between siblings is excused as normal sexual exploration between two young people although the long-term effects of sibling incest are just as damaging as adult/child incest (Wiehe, 1997). However, researchers such as Johnson and Feldmeth (1993) suggest that specific categories of juvenile child abusers exist. Those categories include the sexually reactive child who has been sexually abused herself/himself and engages in sex with other children not through force or coercion but under the premise of sexual exploration (Johnson &

Feldmeth,1993). In incestuous families with multiple child victims, a sexually reactive child is common.

In cases of sibling incest, there is generally one aggressive partner and one submissive partner. Specifically, if the older sibling has more knowledge or experience, he/she is usually the aggressor and the younger sibling is usually the victim (Wiehe, 1997). Explanations of sibling incest include not only an attempt by one sibling to control or humiliate the other (Laviola, 1992), but also the fact that many of these juvenile abusers have been abused themselves and by abusing other children in the family they are attempting to understand what they have experienced. Unfortunately, as the shame of incest is a rationale to keep silent, the victim has no means by which to end the abuse (Tsun, 1999). In many cases, sibling incest continues until the victim ends the abuse.

Extrafamilial Abuse

In extrafamilial abuse, the perpetrator is someone outside of the family. The abusers who target children often do so under the context of a social relationship with the child (Crosson-Tower, 2002). Just as an adult male may frequent a nightclub to meet an adult female, the child abuser (or molester) places himself/herself in the proximity of children. These offenders include neighbors, schoolteachers, Sunday school teachers, Little League coaches, members of the clergy, and strangers. Surprising to many people and contrary to the theory of "stranger danger" is the fact that fewer that one-half of the cases of child sexual assaults are extrafamilial (Crosson-Tower, 1999; Clark, 1999). In fact, it is now recognized that many of those who sexually abuse children are actually known to (acquaintances of) the child and his/her family. Often these cases of extrafamilial abuse (acquaintances or strangers) involve sexual addicts, pedophiles, child pornography, and child sex rings.

Sexual Addicts. Just as a drug addict adopts a delusional thought process to rationalize his behavior and belief system, the sexual addict adopts a distorted belief to support his ob-session (Crosson-Tower, 1999), the sexual abuse of children. The sexual addict, preoccupied with the thought of sex, plans the abuse and then executes the plan. Unfortunately, in these cases the victims of the sex addict are children. However, in most cases of child sexual assault, the perpetrator is not clas-sified as a sexual addict.

Pedophiles. According to Wallace (1999), pedophilia is sexual fixation by an adult on the thought of a sexual encounter with a young child. Numerous studies have been conducted on pedophilia; however, most support the notion that just as an adult female may be attracted to a male that is 6'2" with blond hair and blue eyes, a pedophile is attracted to certain physical characteristics of a child. One particular type of ped-ophilia is pederasty; this refers to the sexual activity of anal intercourse and often involves a boy (Radbill, 1968).

In a 1987 study of 561 sex offenders, it was reported that pedophiles who targeted young boys outside of the home committed the greatest number of crimes, with each of-fender reporting an average of over 150 child victims (Abel, 1987). This repetitive behavior of pedophiles makes cases involving these individuals far easier to investigate than cases involving *situational child molesters* or those cases where the child was a victim of opportunity (Lanning, 1992).

Much of the research on the subject of pedophiles and situational child molesters, suggests that pedophiles molest many more children than the situational molester (or those molesters who abuse children because they are available). However, explaining the behavior is often difficult. In the in-vestigation of a sexual assault by a pedophile or a preferen-tial child molester, one must recognize that just as an adult male may complete a series of steps or stages in the "court-ing" of an adult female, a pedophile also often completes a series of steps in the process of molesting a child. As dis-cussed under the concept of Victim Precipitation Theory in Chapter 2, the victim exhibits some behavior or personal characteristic that encourages the attacker. In the case of child sexual abuse by a preferential child molester, the child, because of his/her physical characteristics, attracts the pedophile.

Pornography. Although illegal in most states, the production and distribution of child pornography is another type of sexual abuse (McCabe, 2000). With improved technology and the increased use of the Internet, the cases of child pornography have multiplied (OVC, 2001). Some sex offenders use the privacy of the Internet to identify those vulnerable children who use the Internet unsupervised (Medaris & Girouard, 2002). Despite federal and state laws prohibiting the transmission of child pornography over the Internet, child porn is still often found there (Mehta & Plaza, 1997). In some cases adults coerce and/or manipulate children to pose or perform sexual acts with those adults, other adults, other children, or alone. However, in many instances, physical contact between the child and the perpetrator never occurs. In fact, in today's advancing technological environment, innocent pictures or images of children may be digitally transformed into pornographic materials, and, in fact, many of the children who appear in the electronically distributed pornography never realize that they have been victimized (OVC, 2001). In the cases of child pornography that involve a real child and sexual abuse, the children are victimized during the production of the pornography and then are repeatedly victimized as the pornography is distributed to the hundreds of viewers in the market for child pornography. At one time, the stereotypical distributor of child pornography was a middle-aged, uneducated, white male. Today, an ever-increasing number of teens and individuals in their twenties are involved in producing and distributing child pornography (Rosenwald, 2002).

Sex Rings. Finally, another type of extrafamilial sexual abuse involves the use of child sex rings. The term sex ring refers to the situation in which one or more offenders are simultaneously involved in the sexual abuse of several children (Lanning,

1992). Therefore, the operation of a sex ring brings a different set of dynamics to child sexual abuse than the "typical" familiar or extrafamiliar cases. A sex ring is a business, in particular, the business of child prostitution. Just as an adult may pay to have consensual sex with an adult partner, adults pay or trade children to satisfy their desire to have sex with a child. The difference in these cases lies in the fact that the child does not have the option of consent (either because of age or ability to distinguish right from wrong). In child sex rings, there is an interaction among multiple victims and multiple offenders. In fact, there is often communication among the offenders in regard to the demographic characteristics of the child and the sex ringleader's ability to locate the sought-after child (Lanning, 1992). Often children who are victims of child sex rings are passed from abuser to abuser; thus, they are victimized over and over again.

Child Victims

There are no clear-cut indicators of risk for child sexual abuse; however, it has been suggested that social isolation of the child and/or family is a major contributor (Crosson-Tower, 1999). In fact, it has been suggested that a child without the avenue of outside contact is especially vulnerable to incest.

Another risk factor is the presence of a stepfather in the home (Finkelhor, 1984). The presence of a stepfather, in many cases, indicates a risk because other men are likely to be in the home. Whether the men are boyfriends of the mother prior to her remarriage or male friends of the current stepfather, the risk to the child for sexual abuse is increased. Simply stated, because most reported perpetrators of sexual abuse are male, additional males increase the likelihood of an incident(s) of sexual abuse.

Finally, the mother's history also plays into the formula of risk. Specifically, if the mother was herself a victim of child sexual abuse, then her child, perhaps at the hands of the same abuser, may also be at risk for victimization (Faller,

1988). If the mother is now a victim of domestic violence that includes sexual violence, the child may be at risk for sexual violence. In addition, if the mother is absent from the home a great deal of the time, if the child is supervised by many different individuals or is left unsupervised, the child's risk for sexual abuse may be increased (Sgroi, 1982; James & Nasjleti, 1983).

Children who are victims of sexual abuse are, in most cases, female. However, in the cases of child sex rings, the victims are more likely to be male (Lanning, 1992). In considering the specific demographic characteristics of abused children, approximately 10% are between the ages of 0 to 3, and approximately 25% are between the ages of 4 to 7 (Finkelhor & Ormrod, 2001). Males are more often victimized at a younger age, while females are more often victimized at an older age. The most vulnerable age for sexual abuse is between the ages of 7 and 13; however, because of an inability to report, as language skills are limited, conclusions on those children under the age of 6 are limited (Crosson-Tower, 1999). In addition, females are more likely to be abused by family members, and males are more likely to be abused by those individuals outside of the family. Finally, children with disabilities (physical or emotional) are at increased risk for sexual abuse (DeYoung, 1982).

Indicators of Abuse

Just as in the case of child physical abuse, there are also physical and behavioral signs or indicators of child sexual abuse. However, in cases of sexual abuse, the behavioral indicators may provide the first clues of abuse to law enforcement or social services investigators.

Physical Indicators

Unfortunately, in most cases of child sexual abuse there are no physical indicators. This is, in part, because the child does not report the abuse immediately after it occurs; thus, any sort of physical evidence is gone (either washed away or healed). In addition, most perpetrators of child sexual abuse do not leave evidence in terms of sperm, blood, or tears in the child's genital area because, in most cases of child sexual assault, vaginal or anal penetration does not occur. However, there are some clear indicators of child sexual abuse.

The first indicator of sexual assault is physical evidence if it is collected immediately after the incident. Other indicators of child sexual assault are the presence of a sexually transmitted disease (STD), especially in cases of young children, and a child's preoccupation with touching his/her genital areas. A fourth indicator, just as in the case of physical abuse, is the presence of suspicious bruises (either in shape or location) on the child. In addition and in reaction to the sexual abuse, the child may attempt to injure himself or herself either through self-mutilation, anorexia, or bulimia (Helfer & Kempe, 1987). Finally, a child with very poor hygiene may be a victim of sexual abuse. These children, in attempts to make themselves less attractive to their perpetrator, will often refuse to bathe, hoping to discourage future sexual assaults. In cases where there exists no physical evidence (the majority of the cases), one must consider the behavioral evidence or indicators.

Behavioral Indicators

Oftentimes a child who is sexually abused will provide hints of that abuse by behavioral instead of physical indicators. In particular, a child who is a victim of sexual abuse may avoid others (especially adults), appear angry, anxious, depressed, or display a drastic personality change (Helfer & Kempe, 1987). The child may experience problems at school in terms of attention, progress, and respect to authority figures. It is not unusual for the victim of sexual abuse to use sexual language or descriptions of sexual acts in conversations that are not considered age appropriate (i.e., a first grader might discuss sexual intercourse and include the mechanics of position and ejaculation) (Wallace, 1999). In addition, it is not unusual for children who are sexually abused to imitate their abusers and sexually abuse other children. Finally, some child victims of sexual abuse indicate fears of everyday activities or an over-estimation of world dangers (Briere & Elliott, 1994) as well as a fear of homosexuality (more the case for male victims) and the fear of being perceived as "damaged goods" (more the case for female victims) (Helfer & Kempe, 1987). These children may appear nervous or stressed out and express the desire to be alone or in a quiet non-interacting environment. The more frequent and severe the sexual abuse, the more obvious the behavioral indicators.

Progression of Sexual Abuse

In attempting to understand the dynamics behind the sexual abuse of children, one must first consider the state of the abuser's mind before the seduction of a child. Finkelhor (1984) suggested that before a sexual assault of a child occurs, there is a progression of stages (or conditions) which must be completed. There are four preconditions to a sexual assault: Precondition I: Motivation to Sexually Abuse; Precondition II: Overcoming Internal Inhibitors; Precondition III: Factors Predisposing to Overcome External Inhibitors; and, Precondition IV: Factors Predisposing to Overcome a Child's Resistance (Finkelhor, 1984).

In Precondition I, the perpetrator or abuser attempts to relate to the child on an emotional level. In this stage, the child is seen as the source of sexual satisfaction for the abuser; other forms of sexual satisfaction such as adults are not available (Finkelhor, 1984). It is during this stage that many perpetrators perceive the everyday actions of the child to be seductive (Crosson-Tower, 1999). A child who sits on the perpetrator's lap or smiles at the perpetrator is perceived as "flirting" with his soon-to-be abuser; thus, the abuser responds with attention to the child. In this stage, the adult is socially comfortable. The adult, perhaps because of his inability to relate to adults on a social or emotional level, enjoys the company of children more than the company of adults.

In Precondition II, the perpetrator must overcome internal inhibitors or his conscious feeling that sex with children is wrong before the sexual abuse will occur (Finkelhor, 1984). It is during this stage that alcohol, drugs, and perhaps pornography will be introduced. Through the use of alcohol, drugs, or the viewing of child pornography, the abuser's internal inhibitors are overcome, and the perpetrator may now focus on overcoming the child's resistance.

It is during Precondition III that the perpetrator must overcome the external inhibitors of a child (Finkelhor, 1984). The goal is to have a willing or at least a non-resisting child victim. Before abuse will occur, the child must consent. The child's internal inhibitors or the perpetrator's external inhibitors must be eliminated. Those external inhibitors may be the amount of supervision of the child or the child's social support system. A child with little adult supervision or without the foundation of someone to confide in is the ideal child for a sexual assault.

Precondition IV is the final stage prior to the sexual abuse of the child. The factors that eliminate the child's resistance are the focus of the perpetrator (Finkelhor, 1984). Whether creating an environment of powerlessness or a trusting relationship between the perpetrator and the child, the abuser must develop an atmosphere to eliminate the child's resistance to sexual activities with the adult. As the abuser places himself in a pseudo-caretaker role for the child, he becomes indispensable in that child's eyes. In turn, the child wants to please that adult and, in most cases, will do all that is asked by the abuser. Once this stage has been satisfied, the child's sexual assault will likely occur.

Consequences of Sexual Abuse

Although the behavioral indicators mentioned are signs of immediate sexual abuse, they can also be long-term consequences of sexual abuse. Other long-term consequences of sexual abuse that have been identified in research include sexual dysfunction (Wiehe, 1997; Duncan & Williams,

1998), an interest in sex with children (Briere & Elliott, 1994), female physical ailments such as chronic pelvic infections and pregnancy complications, and injuries related to the abuse (Grimstad & Schei, 1997). Despite the fact that some states now restrict civil claims from sexual abuse victims to those filed before the accuser turns 21 (Shane, 2002), victims of child sexual abuse, once they reach adulthood, often find themselves unable to understand and participate in a "normal" adult sexual relationship. The same is true for adult victims of rape in that a rape affects their abilities to enjoy a healthy sexual relationship; a child introduced to sex through the avenue of abuse has no "norm" of behavior and, thus, is limited in his/her abilities to participate in an adult relationship.

Another long-term consequence of child sexual abuse is domestic violence (Bynum & Thompson, 2002; Brown & Finkelhor, 1986). Whether the adult plays the role of the victim (as most women do) in the domestic setting or the abuser, the issues of power and control evident in their childhood victimization are again present in their adulthood.

Alcohol and drug abuse have also been linked to child sexual abuse (Brown & Finkelhor, 1986). The alcoholic and the drug addict, through the use of these substances, can escape (if only for a little while) their memories of abuse. Unfortunately, in many cases, the alcohol or drugs are not sufficient and suicide is the result.

Finally, delinquency and crime have been asserted to be an effect of child sexual abuse (Bartollas, 2000). Prostitution, drug abuse, sexual assaults, and parricide (murder of one's parents) often reveal child sexual abuse (Wallace, 1999). Today the majority of the convicted offenders in prison report child abuse and neglect. Many of the violent offenders have a history of sexual abuse (Barkan, 2001). For prostitutes on the street, selling their body is no different from the sexual abuse they experienced as a child. However, the notion of self-control on the part of the prostitute allows prostitution to be seen as a better scenario than child victimization.

Criminal Justice Responses

Just as in the cases of child physical abuse, the responses by the criminal justice system to child sexual abuse have varied over time and by region within the United States. Historically, from a legal standpoint, responses to child sexual assault have been very reactive to a particular case of child sexual abuse.

In 1994, the Jacob Wetterling Act provided the first legislative initiative to establish a sex offender registry after young Jacob was abducted. At that time there was no comprehensive list of possible offenders from which law enforcement officers could begin their investigation. In 1996, Megan's Law amended the Wetterling Act to include a community notification system when a released sex offender moved into a new area where the residents are not familiar with his history. In 2000, the Wetterling Act was again amended to the Campus Sex Crimes Prevention Act, according to which convicted sex offenders who wish to enroll in institutes of higher learning must submit their criminal records to the college or university.

To address the issue of pornography and computer technology, the 1977 Sexual Exploitation of Children Act prohibited the transportation of child pornography by mail or computer. In 1984, the Child Protection Act defined anyone younger than 18 as a child. In 1988, the Child Protection Enforcement Act made it unlawful to use a computer to transport child pornography and provided a specific age definition of a child based upon the physical characteristics of the child, and, in 1996, the Child Pornography Act amended the definition of a child to include computer-generated children (McCabe, 2000). Unfortunately, in 2002, the Supreme Court ruled that computer-generated children were not actually children.

From a law enforcement and prosecution standpoint, these laws provide the avenue for their investigations. In particular, Megan's Law provides law enforcement the ability to detain known sex offenders in the event of a missing or sexually assaulted child. U.S. courts, with the exception of the matter of computer-generated children, have been, for the most part, accommodating of the legislation against child sexual abuse. In the case of *US v. Reedy* (1988), the Supreme Court supported the conviction of a stepfather charged with taking pornographic pictures of two young girls. A Task Force program sponsored by the Internet Crimes Against Children (ICAC) provides citizens with an avenue for reporting the use of the Internet by child molesters to solicit children (Medaris & Girouard, 2002).

From a corrections standpoint, those convicted of child sexual abuses are generally the most victimized group of inmates within the prison system. Efforts are being made every day to rehabilitate convicted child sex offenders, generally under the categories of re-education, resocialization, behavior modification, and counseling (Pollock, 1997). In addition, convicted sex offenders, under the umbrella of rehabilitation, have received chemotherapy or DepoProvera (a female hormone) (Pollock). Unfortunately, much of the research on sex offenders concludes that rehabilitation has not been successful (Furby, Weinrott & Blackshaw, 1989).

Conclusion

Child sexual abuse includes fondling a child's genitals, intercourse, incest, rape, sodomy, and the exploitation of children through pornography or prostitution (ACF, 1999). Despite recent attempts by state and local authorities to end the sexual abuse of children, it continues. In fact, it is estimated that over 200,000 incidents of child sexual abuse occur in this county on an annual basis (Sedlak & Broadhurst, 1996).

Questions

1. What is the definition of child sexual abuse, and what actions are included in child sexual abuse?

2. Who are the perpetrators of child sexual abuse in terms of their familial and extrafamilial relationships to the child or children?
3. What is pedophilia?
4. What are some of the physical and behavioral indicators of child sexual abuse?
5. What is the progression in terms of existing conditions in the seduction of a child?

Questions for Thought

1. Given the fact that most of the cases of sexual abuse of children occur within the family, is not child sexual abuse more of a family issue rather than a community issue?
2. Computer-generated children are not really children. Is there then a problem with using computer-generated images in child pornography?
3. Under all circumstances, is child pornography wrong? Why?
4. In many cases, the sexual abuse of a child is explained by opportunity. Does the fact that the abuse occurred simply because the adult was, say, intoxicated and looking for sexual gratification make a difference?
5. If the sexual abuse of children is so damaging to children over the long-term, why are there not harsher penalties for convicted offenders?

SEXUAL ABUSE

In October of 1993, 12-year-old Polly Klaas was kidnapped from a slumber party in her bedroom while the other children watched in fear. In June of 1996, Richard Allen Davis was convicted of her murder after he led police to her body. In this case there existed evidence of not only murder but also sexual abuse. In September of 1996, Davis was sentenced to death within California's state prison of San Quentin. After the death of Polly Klaas, her father initiated Klaas Kids, a not-for-profit organization that produces and distributes information on the protection of children.

CHAPTER 4

EMOTIONAL ABUSE

Research supports the notion that the most common form of abuse is emotional abuse (Wallace, 1999). However, emotional abuse is often difficult to document and prove; therefore, many cases of emotional abuse go undetected and unaddressed (Crosson-Tower, 1999). For anyone who is uncertain as to whether they have ever witnessed emotional abuse, observe a 2-year-old child being "verbally disciplined" by her parents for acting tired and cranky while the parents finish their dinner in a restaurant at 10 p.m. or observe a child as he is told by his caretaker that he is "too dumb" to understand a particular toy that he/she wants the parent to purchase.

Researchers conclude that emotional abuse is perhaps the most damaging form of abuse in terms of long-term consequences; the phrase "cuts go away but words do not" illustrates the long-lasting effect of emotional abuse. It is unfortunate that court cases based simply upon emotional abuse are nonexistent. Prosecutors who wish to gain convictions of child abuse would rather pursue a case of physical or sexual abuse.

This chapter includes a discussion of the various types of emotional abuse, the indicators of emotional abuse, the perpetrators of emotional abuse, two theoretical explanations for emotional abuse, and criminal justice responses to emotional abuse.

Over the last decade, the reported number of cases involving emotional abuse have increased by over 200% (Sedlak & Broadhurst, 1996) with children from single-parent homes and children of families with annual incomes lower than $15,000 identified as at higher risk for emotional abuse than children from two-parent homes or children of more affluent families (Sedlack & Broadhurst). The difference in most

> Emotional abuse is a pattern of psychologically destructive behavior targeted toward a child or children (Gabarino, Guttman & Seeley, 1986). Included under the category of emotional abuse are isolation, terrorizing, ignoring, and corruption of the child (Crosson-Tower, 1999).

cases of emotional abuse as compared to the cases of physical abuse or sexual abuse lies in the fact that emotional abuse often accompanies other forms of abuse and is rarely seen as the only form of abuse that the child experiences. A child who suffers emotional abuse is often also physically abused, sexually abused, or neglected. Emotional abuse can range from a child being belittled or ridiculed to a caretaker using methods of confinement such as placing the child in a closet or trunk for hours (Kelley, Thornberry & Smith, 1997). Just as there are varying degrees of emotional abuse, there are also varying consequences to emotional abuse. However, one must first consider the types of emotional abuse.

Types of Emotional Abuse

In general, there are six different types of emotional abuse: (1) rejection; (2) isolation; (3) terrorizing (or verbal abuse);

(4) ignoring; (5) corrupting; and (6) destroying personal property. Each type carries with it its own set of dynamics and consequences.

Rejection

In regard to rejection, many parents either subconsciously or consciously decide to reject their child or children. For most individuals, the concept of a parent refusing the love of their children is unimaginable; however, there are many parents who reject their children and many reasons for a parent to do so. For example, a mother may have her own vision of the perfect pregnancy and birth. This vision may be destroyed during the pregnancy. A mother who has experienced difficulties in pregnancy, labor, and/or delivery may blame the child for not providing the expected "wonderful" scenario and may, in turn, transfer that blame by rejecting of that child.

In another explanation of rejection, the child is rejected by one parent because he/she possesses characteristics similar to the spouse. It is not uncommon for couples, once in love, now to hate each other. A parent who has formed a dislike to a spouse or ex-spouse may also reject the child who resembles the spouse. The child, simply because he/she looks like the former partner, is rejected by a parent. Finally there are those parents who decide, after the child is born, that parenting is not for them. These parents then refuse to acknowledge the child or make adjustments in their lifestyle for that child; hence, the child, simply because he/she exists is rejected.

Isolation

The isolation of a child involves the adult cutting the child off from other social interactions such as grandparents, siblings, or even friends (Crosson-Tower, 1999) and is another form of emotional abuse. Some parents, because of a need to control that child or an exaggerated fear of victimization, will isolate the child from others. In addition to the social isolation, in many cases, a parent who suffers from some sort of mental illness will be incapable of socially interacting with the child; thus, the child is isolated from not only everyone else but also the parent. Often, children who have been isolated begin to fear others, and, despite the fact that the caretaker has caused the isolation, the children become totally dependent upon their abuser and desire only to be in the company of that caretaker. In these types of cases of emotional abuse, children will often resist the interventions of law enforcement or social services and aggressively display love and attachment to their parent(s). In reality, the child views even a bad parent as better than no parent at all.

Terrorizing

Another type of emotional abuse is terrorizing in which the adult verbally assaults the child to create a climate of fear (Crosson-Tower, 1999). Many children are terrorized. A caretaker who uses verbal threats either directly aimed at the child or at other members of the family (as in the case of spousal abuse) maintains a climate of fear and produces a frightened child. In turn, this terrorizing creates a stifling and hostile environment for the child. Just as the intimidation of an adult is a crime, the intimidation of a child, even at the hands of his/her caretaker, is considered a crime (McCabe & Gregory, 1997). Often, in these cases, the child views the world as hostile and rejects any initiatives from others outside of the home. These children live in fear of their abusers—fear of victimization and fear of failing to please that abuser. If one can imagine the constant strain of being in an environment with some element that produces fear, one can imagine the emotional abuse of the terrorized child.

Ignoring

Ignoring a child, when applied to the child's basic needs of food and shelter, may be referred to as neglect (Wallace, 1999). However, when a child is deprived of social stimulation and responsiveness from his/her caretaker, it is classified as emotional abuse (Crosson-Tower, 1999). Children who are ignored usually either seek social relationships where they can be non-responsive or social relationships where they can be the center of attention. Children who are ignored, in many cases, become unmotivated to achieve any sort of recognition and, therefore, simply exist without the curiosity or exploration most equated with childhood. Later in life, these children may turn to drugs and alcohol to maintain that isolation from peers and family members. In other cases, children who are ignored seek love and attention from individuals other than their caretaker. In some cases, this search for outside attention results in sexual promiscuity or even the sexual abuse of the child at the hands of neighbors or acquaintances of the family. The parent, who has little time for the child, perhaps because of employment pressures or problems with substance abuse, ignores the child. Adult human beings seek and desire social relationships. Children also seek and desire such relationships. If the child's desire for a relationship is not satisfied in the home, the child will seek a satisfactory relationship outside of the home.

Corruption

The corruption of a child involves engaging the child in destructive and sometime criminal behaviors and is also a type of emotional abuse (Crosson-Tower, 1999). Some of the most common forms of corruption include providing the child the opportunity to use illegal drugs and alcohol, enticement of a child into the selling of illegal drugs, and child prostitution organized through an adult. Unfortunately for the child, one long-term consequence for such abuse is premature death. In addition, one of the newest areas of child corruption from a law enforcement standpoint involves child pornography over the Internet (McCabe, 2000). In many cases, the children who are depicted in pornographic images over the Internet are enticed or seduced into the activity through the use of drugs, alcohol, and adult pornography. Over time, children who have been corrupted by an adult often display antisocial and violent behaviors (Bartollas, 2000; Bynum & Thompson, 2002). These child victims of corruption become the perpetrators of criminal actions (Barkan, 2001).

Property Destruction

Finally, child emotional abuse may be manifested in the destruction of a child's property or pets (Wiehe, 1997). Although more commonly seen in abuse by a sibling and not originally recognized as a form of emotional abuse, the destruction of a child's prized possession or the child's pet can be devastating to the child, especially when this is done in view of the child. Many individuals, to enforce their notion of control over the child, will injure or kill the child's pet. The child, who witnesses the act, feels guilty for not only being unable to stop the abuse but also for being "responsible" for the action. Hence the child is powerless against their abuser.

Indicators of Emotional Abuse

Just as in cases of physical and sexual abuse, there are no clear-cut indicators of emotional abuse. However, there are some recognizable ones based upon the personality or personality changes of the child. Emotionally abused children often display extreme behaviors from very happy to manically depressed. They often suffer from eating disorders and substance abuse and exhibit almost a compulsion toward details (Crosson-Tower, 2002). Socially and educationally, emotionally abused children will often interact cruelly with others, are often socially withdrawn, and often exhibit learning disabilities (Crosson-Tower).

Perpetrators of Emotional Abuse

With the exception of child corruption, most cases of child emotional abuse involve the parents or caretakers of the child. Explanations of the motives of these perpetrators include problems of mental capacity, personality, family upbringing, and family environment. Those parents or caretakers with mental illness are unable to fully understand the dynamics of their relationships with their children; thus, emotional abuse occurs. In addition, some parents or caretakers, because of internal emotional battles, abuse their child or children. For example, in the case of a mother who is very career minded, project immersed, or simply battling an identify crisis of "mom" versus "me" children can be emotionally ignored for hours or days. One cannot discount the fact that many parents, although they entered into parenthood with the best intentions, do not enjoy being a parent. These individuals have often had little experience with young children and are uncomfortable in adult-child relationships. Therefore, they view parenting in a negative light, with interactions with their children founded in the authority of their positions in the family.

If a parent's own needs were not met in childhood, resulting in emotional abuse, the cycle of abuse continues, as the parent is now emotionally abusive to his/her children (O'Hagan, 1993). In addition, parents who suffer from substance abuse or have experienced an unwanted pregnancy may be emotionally abusive to their child or children. Finally, parents who have a child who is mentally or physically handicapped also tend to emotionally abuse that child. Childrearing, in itself, is difficult. Add to that the difficulty of caring for a child with special needs, and the strain of parenting becomes greater. Also, in some cases, perpetrators of child emotional abuse find themselves in unfortunate situations such as unemployment or marital disarray. In these cases, parents may be disillusioned with their spouses and may transfer those feelings of hostility toward the spouse to the child or children of the spouse (Covitz, 1986; Klosinski, 1993).

Finally, one cannot discount the emotional abuse of a child at the hands of a sibling. Siblings, just as they may be the perpetrators of sexual and physical abuse, can emotionally abuse each other (Hardy, 2001). In most cases, the emotional abuse among siblings is from older sibling to younger. However, there are incidents of younger siblings terrorizing older siblings; this is especially the case in a mentally or physically disabled older sibling. These siblings require more attention, and unfortunately, this often causes jealousy from siblings; thus, these children are more prone to sibling emotional abuse.

Theoretical Explanations

Although the theories of the Cycle of Violence, Psychodynamic Model, and Environmental Stress Model discussed in chapter 2 may also apply to emotional abuse, other theoretical explanations for emotional abuse include but are not limited to the Funnel of Violence and Social Learning Theory.

Funnel of Violence

Under the theory of the *Funnel of Violence,* emotional abuse is explained as an outcome of the living conditions of the abuser. Specifically, individuals who live in violence are able to filter or reduce the levels of violence through their families and peers (Wolfe, Wekerle, Reitzel-Jaffe, Grasley, Pittman & MacEachran, 1997). At the mouth of the funnel are the everyday influences of violence; the functions of family and peers filter or reduce the influences of violence (Wolfe, Wekerle, Reitzel-Jaffe, Grasley, Pittman & MacEachran). At the end of the funnel is the only remaining element of violence, which for our purposes is emotional abuse. Thus, the more violent the culture of the child, the more likely that violence, in terms of emotional abuse, will remain in the socialization of the child.

Social Learning

Under the context of the theory of *Social Learning,* the media and the general culture influence the behavior of the individuals (Miedzian, 1995; Barongan & Hall, 1995). Popular family television shows depict emotional abuse or sarcasm from parents toward the child members of the household, and these shows influence the behaviors of the family viewers. After viewing the show, families may begin modeling the actors and abuse occurs. Emotional abuse is one outcome of modeling these behaviors or social learning.

Criminal Justice Responses

As stated at the beginning of this chapter, the criminal justice system does not respond to child emotional abuse unless the emotional abuse exists along with physical abuse, sexual abuse, or neglect. However, just as there are children who suffer from multiple forms of child abuse, there are children who are victims of simple emotional abuse.

As emotional abuse leaves no physical evidence, and the opinions of whether or not someone was emotionally abusive to a child vary by individuals and circumstances, the victims of emotional abuse are unrecognized by the criminal justice system. In these cases, as there exists no evidence to support an investigation by law enforcement officials, the children are left to overcome their victimizations themselves. Without an initial investigation by law enforcement or some officiating social services agency, the court systems will not become involved. Since law enforcement is not involved in the case, the incidents of emotional abuse remain undocumented and therefore unaddressed.

Conclusion

Some students of child abuse view emotional abuse as most damaging to the child. Whether emotional abuse was simply a part of the child's sexual and physical abuse or whether it is the only form of abuse, children who have experienced emotional abuse are often withdrawn and continue that antisocial behavior as adults. Since emotional abuse is viewed as not leaving any permanent scars, it often goes unnoticed by the victim and society (Crosson-Tower,

1999). The child victim of emotional abuse is the most likely to continue the pattern of abuse as an adult. Specifically, the child victim, when an adult, may choose a spouse who is emotionally abusive, and, in turn, these former victims of emotional abuse now continue that emotional abuse with their children.

Despite efforts at the state and local level to reduce the incidents of child abuse, the numbers continue to increase. Most researchers and practioners view emotional abuse as the most common type of abuse and the most severe type of abuse in terms of long-term consequences; however, there have been few efforts by society to end emotional abuse. Unfortunately, as with any cycle of abuse, unless proactive efforts are implemented, the abuse continues.

Questions

1. What is the definition of child emotional abuse, and how does it differ from the other forms of child abuse?
2. What specific actions are included in the category of emotional abuse?
3. What are some of the indicators of child emotional abuse?
4. From an abuser's perspective, can you explain child emotional abuse?
5. How can one explain, from a theoretical perspective, child emotional abuse?

Questions for Thought

1. Of all of the types of emotional abuse, rejection, isolation, terrorizing, ignoring, corrupting, or destroying personal property, which do you feel is most detrimental?
2. As a prosecutor, if you had the choice to prosecute a case of emotional abuse by rejection verses a case of emotional abuse by terrorizing, which would you choose? Why?

3. Are there other theoretical models to explain emotional abuse than the Cycle of Violence, the Psychodynamic Model, the Environmental Stress Model, the Funnel of Violence, and Social Learning Theory?
4. Why are more law enforcement efforts not aimed at reducing emotional abuse?
5. Does child emotional abuse really exist or is it simple unkindness to a child?

CHAPTER 5

NEGLECT

A child is rushed to the hospital and is pronounced dead after being left in a locked car with an estimated temperature over 120° for over three hours while a mother shops. A toddler dies as a result of a fall when he crawls out of a second story open window of his home. A child who, because of a physical disability, is unable to feed himself dies of starvation at the hands of his caregivers. All of these scenarios are examples of child neglect.

Many researchers believe that neglect, or a failure to provide for some basic need of a child, is one of the most common forms of child abuse. Although society has advanced in many ways in addressing child abuse, neglect, which is related to the care of our children, has not been an area that has kept pace with those advances. Parents still fail to seek medical assistance, provide proper nutritional meals, and ensure that their children attend school. Whether it is explained as ignorance on the part of parents or callousness, many individuals in America today feel that there is some degree of responsibility on the part of society to protect all children.

Of all the categories of child abuse, neglect has probably received the least amount of attention from researchers. The reasons for this lack of attention include the fact that neglect is not seen as important or as detrimental to the child. Another reason is that neglect is less dramatic and fails in the shock factor that is often required to "STOP ABUSE" (Gabarino & Collins, 1999). Neglect does not lend itself to a quick solution or short-term evaluations of success. Finally, addressing neglect involves a long process of teaching parents to identify, first, the basic needs of a child and then avenues for satisfying those basic needs (Crosson-Tower, 2002); thus, researchers interested in empirical assessments, opt for another category of abuse. However, this does not infer that neglect is less important.

It has been estimated that nearly 60% of all child victims of physical, sexual, and emotional abuse are also victims of neglect and that more child deaths from maltreatment or abuse are associated with neglect than any other type of abuse (ACF, 1999; Helfer & Kempe, 1987). In addition, it is estimated that over one-half of the child abuse cases reported to law enforcement agencies within the United States are cases of neglect (Kelley, Thornberry & Smith, 1997).

Neglect is defined as a parent or caretaker's failure to provide the basic needs of survival for a child (Bartollas, 2000). Child neglect may be but is not limited to the areas of supervision, physical care, emotional care, and education.

This chapter discusses the types of neglect: physical, educational, emotional, and supervision as well as some of the indicators of child neglect. Also discussed in this chapter are the causes of neglect, the consequences of child neglect, and responses by the criminal justice system to neglect.

At some point in their lives, all children

may feel that they are neglected—the child whose parents miss his ballgame, the child who did not receive a particular present for her birthday, the child who is left alone in the home for 20 minutes while the parents visit the neighbors, or the child who makes his own breakfast. However, most practioners would not identify those cases as neglect. In fact, due to the necessity of evidence, the most common category of neglect addressed by law enforcement and social services is physical neglect (Crosson-Tower, 2002). All children are potential victims of neglect; however, certain children have been identified as being at higher risk. In general, boys are at a higher risk for physical neglect than girls (Sedlak & Broadhurst, 1996). In considering the family characteristics of neglected children, children of single parents are at an 87% greater risk of physical neglect than children of two-parent families. Children in large families are more likely to be victims of physical neglect, and children from the lowest-income families are more likely victims of educational neglect (Sedlak & Broadhurst, 1996). One must be aware of the fact that there are many types of neglect, with each type addressing a specific area in the child's life.

Types of Neglect

The types of neglect can be divided into four categories: physical, educational, emotional, and supervision. These categories, although appearing mutually exclusive, may overlap in some categories, as most children who are victims of neglect are actually victims of one or more different categories of neglect.

Physical Neglect

By definition, physical neglect refers to the caretaker's inability to reduce or prevent the child's likelihood of physical harm (Crosson-Tower, 1999). This form of neglect includes a refusal to allow or a delay in the seeking of healthcare for the child, failing to provide adequate nutrition for the child, a disregard for the child's personal hygiene and/or an inability to provide a sanitary home for the child, a disregard for the child's safety, and the risk to an unborn child due to the use of drugs and/or alcohol by the mother during pregnancy. In a nutshell, physical neglect addresses the neglect of any part of a child's life that may result in physical injury or illness to that child.

Historically, and from a legal perspective, the most common example of physical neglect is a caretaker's choice to refuse medical treatment of an ill or injured child (Wallace, 1999). In the late 1800s during the *Heinemann's Appeal,* the Supreme Court of Pennsylvania (1880) supported the principle that states may intervene in the best interest of the child when parents fail to provide medical care. Through this ruling, a child does not have to suffer without relief from illness or injury if the parents refuse medical treatment; in these cases, the state may order the treatment of the child.

A failure to provide adequate nutrition and personal hygiene is another example of neglect of common concern for law enforcement and social services. One memoir on the topic of child physical neglect is David Pelzer's (1995) best-selling *A Child Called It*. Pelzer's account of starvation at the hands of his mother brought to the public consciousness the existence of child neglect and the importance of agency intervention.

The medical community has identified a condition called *Non-Organic Failure to Thrive Syndrome* in which a caretaker's not knowing how to properly feed a baby or failing to provide an adequate amount of milk/formula for the baby results in the delayed development of the child or in some cases the death of the child (English, 1978). Failure to Thrive recognizes that all neglect is not intentional; however, with or without intent, the outcome for a neglected child may be death. Failure to Thrive also constitutes physical neglect.

The failure to maintain a safe home, to "baby-proof" a home, or to ensure that a child utilizes a car safety seat may also constitute neglect. Children may ingest common poisons in the home, fall from the top of staircases, or drown in a couple of inches of bath water. The caretakers who choose not to take the proper precautions to protect their children may face prosecution in family court, and lawsuits can be filed in civil court even though the neglect may not be intentional. In Washington, DC, in November of 2001, the family of a disabled child who died in a Delaware nursing home filed a $120 million suit based upon neglect (Higham & Horwitz, 2001).

Finally, one of the latest concerns is in the area of prenatal care. In particular the failure of a mother to seek prenatal care for her unborn baby and the use of drugs and alcohol by the mother while pregnant may also be reasons for the criminal charge of physical neglect. This is a topic of liability in the criminal courts, and, in many states, the definition of a child has been rewritten to include an unborn child (or fetus).

Educational Neglect

Educational neglect refers to the caretaker's failure to provide an education or a means of education to the child (Crosson-Tower, 1999). Included in this category of neglect are chronic school truancy, a failure to enroll the child in school, and inattention by the parents or caretakers to a child's special education programs. Each of these examples of educational neglect is reason for prosecution in the U.S. court systems.

All children in the United States are required to attend school. In turn, parents are required to register their children for school. In some cases of educational neglect, parents fail to register their children or fail to send their children to school. Thus, as seen from a legal perspective, the parent who fails to ensure that his or her child attends school, is guilty of educational neglect.

Another aspect of educational neglect involves the situation of a mentally challenged child or a child with a learning disability and a parent or caretaker who makes little or no effort to assure that child an education or educational progress (Crosson-Tower, 1999). Their rights as U.S. citizens afford all children the opportunity of education.

Parents are responsible for ensuring that their children seize that opportunity.

Emotional Neglect

The emotional neglect of children may be, in the case of threats or intimidation, classified as emotional abuse. However, for the purpose of this discussion *emotional neglect* includes inadequate nurturance and affection, the abuse of another person in the presence of the child, and a refusal to provide psychological care by the parent or caretaker (NCCAN, 1993). Child development consists of a series of stages, and each stage provides a new or additional set of circumstances for the emotionally neglected child. The child who is not nurtured and shown affection but simply ignored has an unstable foundation for a "normal" relationship. The child who never experiences positive contacts between parent and child, is unaware of these types of relationships and, in many cases, is unable to initiate the process of bonding with other individuals.

In some cases of emotional neglect, an older child who did not receive the love and attention from his/her parents makes a conscious effort to fulfill that role for the younger siblings. In these cases, the child becomes the nurturer and essentially the caretaker to the younger siblings.

In other families where emotional neglect exists, the roles of parent and child are undefined and blurred; thus, the child becomes the nurturer to the parents. However, despite this initiative to maintain family closeness taken by the child, the child usually has little self-value and will often times view himself/herself as not capable of attracting or maintaining a loving relationship. It is not unusual for these children to drift in and out of relationships as adults.

Some researchers view emotional neglect as one of the most damaging phenomena in a child's life (Wallace, 1999; Sudermann & Jaffe, 1997). In addition to the physical condition of Failure to Thrive, which may result from emotional neglect, many researchers have asserted that children who are unloved demonstrate neediness and general feelings of fear of abandonment or rejection later in life (Briere, 1997). These children, who have little value in themselves, often become either the victims or perpetrators of domestic violence (Barkan, 2001).

Supervision Neglect

Neglect, in terms of supervision, is the failure to adequately supervise a child (NCCAN, 1993). Supervision neglect includes abandonment (both long term and short term) as well as the expulsion of the child from his/her residence without providing adequate housing for the child. Also included under this category of supervision neglect is the case of the child who is allowed to stay away from the home overnight or for extended periods of time without the caretaker's knowledge of the child's location (NCCAN). In many cases of supervision neglect, the children will simply leave home and, as the parents/caretakers are not in the habit of attending to their whereabouts, the child (when the parents eventually realize that he/she is gone) is not reported to law enforcement officials as missing or as a runaway (Crosson-Tower, 2002).

Probably one of the most debated hypotheses in the discussion of supervision neglect is the notion that decreased supervision increases the likelihood of delinquency. The notion that unsupervised youths are more likely to be involved in illegal activities (Bynum & Thompson, 2002) or, more generally stated, that inadequate supervision in the home helps to explain delinquent behavior is a common philosophy (Bartollas, 2000). In the absence of caretakers to supervise the child, the child becomes accustomed to acting as he/she desires without thought of the consequences. It is an unfortunate case of a lack of adequate supervision that a child is injured, killed, or inflicts injury upon or kills another person.

Indicators of Neglect

Just as there are many indicators of child physical, sexual, and emotional abuse, there are also many indicators of neglect. School officials are most likely to be involved in identifying a neglected child. In fact, in most states, educators, because of their positions, are mandated reporters of child abuse and neglect and must accept their responsibilities in reporting possible cases of abuse.

Neglect manifests itself in two forms—either physically or through behavioral indicators. However, it must be acknowledged that although the following characteristics are indicators of neglect, they are not always the result of neglect. Just as with any type of child abuse, those investigating such charges should weigh all the facts prior to pronouncing neglect.

Physical Indicators

One of the more common physical indicators of neglect is poor physical development. Research has revealed that neglected children often produce poor growth patterns (Wallace, 1999; Crosson-Tower, 1999). These children will be smaller than other children of the same age, and, a neglected child will often be below the 15th percentile of their growth range for their age and sex. In many cases, related to lack of physical development, a neglected child may appear to be constantly hungry or even to suffer from malnutrition. These children may steal food or hoard food and eat (when they are allowed) as though they are starved. In many cases of neglect, the children are in various stages of starvation. In addition, and as is commonly the case, the child's hygiene is also a good indicator of neglect (Bartollas, 2000). In particular, a child with poor hygiene, a smell of urine, rotten teeth, or head lice and/or unattended physical or medical problems may also be a victim of neglect (Crosson-Tower, 2002).

Finally, in many cases, child neglect produces a child who suffers from constant fatigue or sleepiness. This child, because of lack of food or lack of shelter may seem always tired and in need of sleep. Again, in most cases, the individuals who are in a position to recognize the physical signs of neglect are the child's teachers.

Behavioral Indicators

In many cases, long before the physical indicators of neglect are revealed, the behavioral indicators will be present. A child who lacks self-confidence or self-worth and has poor relationships with peers may be a victim of neglect (Wolfe, McMahon & Peters, 1997). Other behavioral indicators of neglect include begging for food, being socially withdrawn, destructive, and eliciting negative responses to gain attention (Crosson-Tower, 2002). Other behavioral indicators related to the education of the child include being developmentally behind other children in the same age group in the understanding of concepts or the advancement of motor skills, difficulties with language comprehension (as generally their interactions have been through one or two-word statements such as no, get out, or shut up) and overall lower intelligence (Crosson-Tower). Finally, neglected children are often self-destructive, destructive to others or other's property (Wallace, 1999).

In many cases, neglected children are expected to assume the role of caretaker for their younger siblings. A child who appears to be mature for his/her age in actions or who acknowledges responsibilities in the home such as cooking dinner for the family or the bathing of siblings may be neglected. Children who are neglected rarely see school as a necessary part of their lives; therefore, a child who is often tardy or absent from school may also be a victim of neglect. Later, of course, most of these neglected children simply drop out of school completely. Finally, a child who appears to be generally depressed or withdrawn may be a victim of neglect.

Causes of Neglect

Just as the parents are responsible for the care of their children, they are also the most likely source of neglect. However, one cannot discuss neglect by parents or caretakers as simply a result of a failure to fulfill their role. Neglect must be addressed in regard to the dynamics behind the care-taker inability to care for their child. From that perspective, most research would assert that child neglect is a result of three different types of parental and family characteristics: the parent/caretaker's developmental history and personality, the characteristics of the family and child, and environmental influences (Crosson-Tower, 1999).

The first attempt to explain the causes of neglect is from the perspective of the caretaker's own developmental history and personality (Gaudin, 1993). Caretakers themselves who have grown up in an environment of neglect are likely to neglect their children. Just as with other forms of abuse and the Cycle of Violence, neglect is often a generational outcome. These acts of neglect are often a result of the parent not knowing or understanding, for example, that a 3-year-old child is not an appropriate caretaker for an 8-month-old baby (Wolfe, McMahon & Peters, 1997) or not understanding that by leaving a 5-year-old alone in a home overnight or for several days constitutes abandonment (Wallace, 1999). Many of these caretakers were raised in an environment of child "responsibility" and, therefore, see nothing wrong with repeating the pattern.

One must also consider the personality or physical condition of the caretaker in the explanation of neglect. Caretakers, in particular, mothers, who are the most likely perpetrators of neglect, may suffer from depression or have an impulsive personality in which such actions as sleeping for days or their lack of actions such as providing meals for the child may result in child neglect. In addition, some caretakers are apathetic and some are psychotic (Crosson-Tower, 2002). Substance abuse or a mentally disadvantaged caretaker may also promote neglect of the child in the household (Gaudin, 1993). Finally, caretakers who themselves are physically ill may not be able to provide for the child's basic needs; in turn, the child is neglected (Helfer and Kempe, 1987).

The second attempt to explain neglect focuses on the characteristics of the family and the child (Gaudin, 1993).

Just as the personality traits of the caretaker may be used to explain child neglect, so may the personality of the child and the characteristics of the family structure. Just as two adults may have a personality conflict, the child and his/her caretaker may also clash. In addition, children who are introverts (e.g., those who demand little attention) or children who do not have the ability (either because of some physical or mental handicap) to request help from a caretaker are children who may become neglected. Children who are one of many children (especially if they are not the oldest or the youngest) may also be neglected, and children from single-parent homes, simply because of the limitations of time on one parent, may also be victims of neglect (Gaudin, 1993). Finally, children who are members of a family in which domestic violence is present may also be victims of child neglect.

The third explanation of neglect is related to environmental influences or sources of stress outside of the family. Families who are isolated from other family members or the community itself lack all outside resources when it comes to childcare. In these families, the neglect of the children is high risk. Finally, economics is another source of stress on the family (Gaudin, 1993). With both parents working or, in the case of a single-parent household, with the one parent working perhaps multiple jobs, there is little time for the child or children. These children, sometimes referred to in literature as *latchkey children,* are often victims of neglect.

Short- and Long-Term Consequences of Neglect

It is unfortunate that neglect may result in children feeling hungry, in pain, or afraid to be alone; however, there are other consequences of neglect (both short and long term) of which society may not be fully aware. Often neglect manifests itself in actions other than disruptive school behavior or withdrawn personalities. Children who are neglected may suffer from sleep problems, weight loss or weight gain, and poor social relations (Bartollas, 2000). These children may suffer from frequent illnesses or be labeled hypochondriacs (Helfer & Kempe, 1987). The neglected children may turn to drugs or alcohol as an escape from their situation or to promiscuous sexual behavior to gain attention. In addition, neglected children may become runaways or throwaways if their parents decide that their presence in the home is no longer convenient (Bynum & Thompson, 2002).

Later in life, it is not uncommon for neglected children to become adults who are unable to relate to their children or adult partners; thus, they continue the cycle of neglect. They may also be involved in drug or alcohol abuse, which again reduces the likelihood of their positive interactions with their families, or the adults who were neglected as children may partake in violent activities such as crime or domestic violence.

Criminal Justice Responses

Although neglect is included under the 1974 Child Abuse Prevention and Treatment Act, most of the responsibility for addressing child neglect rests with the states and local governments. Many counties and cities, frustrated with the standards of proof necessary in state statues, have initiated county and city ordinances to address neglect. In Omaha City, Nebraska, those who leave children under the age of 7 unattended in vehicles may find themselves facing fines and jail time (*Omaha World Herald*, 2002).

Just as the case with physical, sexual, and emotional abuse, after an incident has been reported, the appropriate child protective services or law enforcement agency will investigate. From a law enforcement perspective, and simply because of the ease of documentation, the easier types of neglect to investigate are physical, educational, and supervision. Emotional neglect (as is the case with emotional abuse) is the most difficult to investigate and document and, unless combined with other types of neglect or other categories of abuse, will probably continue to be "unrecognized" by criminal justice officials.

Conclusion

Child neglect is not a new topic for those whose jobs place them in positions of daily contact with children; however, the problem has no simple solution. In cases of physical, sexual, or emotional abuse, interventions often focus on ending the abuse; however, neglect, because of its underlying dynamics of family structure, personalities, and environmental influences, does not equate with a simple fix.

In the United States, more child fatalities are associated with neglect than any other form of child abuse (ACF, 1999), and most efforts by law enforcement and departments of social services are focused simply upon physical neglect. Only through education and intervention may the problem of child neglect be addressed. Only through interested parties will the problem of child neglect be solved.

Questions

1. What is child neglect, and what are the basic types of child neglect?
2. Why are most of the efforts by law enforcement and social services focused upon physical neglect?
3. What are some of the physical and behavioral indicators of neglect?
4. What are some of the causes of neglect?
5. What are some of the consequences to the child victim of neglect?

Questions for Thought

1. Should parents be held accountable for physical neglect if they are poor?

2. Should parents be held accountable if their children choose not to go to school?
3. If a child runs away, is the parent responsible for that child's well-being?
4. If a child is fed, cleaned, taken to school, and given medical attention when needed, is that child neglected?
5. How could you, in today's society, explain the emotional abuse of a child?

CHAPTER 6

PROTECTING THE CHILD

In today's prisons, most of the offenders convicted of crimes against children are incarcerated for child sexual abuse, and most of those offenders have victimized someone in their families or households (Finkelhor & Ormrod, 2001). In addition, most offenders incarcerated for crimes against children were likely to have reported being victims of either child physical abuse or child sexual abuse (Finkelhor & Ormrod).

From a criminal justice perspective, the subject of child abuse is three-sided. First, the victims, because they are children, are extremely vulnerable in nature. Second, the topic of child abuse often creates a highly charged public reaction (Finkelhor & Ormrod, 2001). Third, without intervention, yesterday's victims may be tomorrow's offenders.

However, child abuse is a subject that law enforcement and other criminal justice entities must address. For law enforcement, the first step in establishing a case of child abuse is the identification of the abuse.

In many cases, the identification of the abuse is based upon behavioral characteristics of the child (Barkan, 2001; Brooks & Weathers, 2001). Therefore, in distinguishing abusive behavior from normal behavior, Finkelhor (1984) suggests that one must consider: (1) if the behavior is age appropriate; (2) how often the behavior occurs; (3) what is the history of the behavior; and (4) if there is an aspect of victimization in the behavior. There may be other possible explanations for the condition of the child than abuse; however, in identified cases of child abuse, intervention is necessary.

This chapter contains information on a general process for removing the abused and/or neglected child from the custody of the parents, on federal actions and legislation that support the protection of children, on strategies by the criminal justice system for preventing abuse today, and a summary of factors for at-risk children.

In any case of child abuse or neglect, the ultimate goal is the protection of the child. States have adopted a process for removing a child from a home or family that endangers the child. In addition, the term "mandatory reporter" is used to identify such individuals as medical personnel, educators, substance abuse counselors, and film processors who, because of their professional capacities and exposure to possible information about children, are mandated by law to report possible cases of child abuse or neglect. Although each state has a statute that specifies the procedures that a mandatory reporter must follow when reporting child abuse or neglect, information reported typically includes the name of the child and parents or guardians, the age of the child, the address of the child, and the nature of the reported abuse. For mandatory reporters who choose not to report a possible case of child abuse, approximately 45 of the states have enacted statutes specifying the penalties for failing to report (*Child Abuse and Neglect State Statutes Elements*, 2000A). In addition, approximately 30 states have enacted state statutes that instruct mandatory reporters to report suspected child deaths to a medical examiner or a coroner, and approximately 15 states have enacted statutes to instruct mandatory reporters to report drug-exposed infants or infant who test positive for drugs (*Child Abuse and Neglect State Statutes Elements*, 2000B).

Removing the Child

Although each state may differ slightly, in general, the process for removing a child from an abusive home is as follows: (1) an initiation of the case; (2) emergency protective custody; (3) probable cause hearing; (4) merits hearing; (5) permanency planning hearing; and (6) termination of parental rights.

Initiation of the Case

Any citizen may initiate an investigation of child abuse or neglect by reporting the event to either a local law enforcement agency or an agency of social services. As stated, mandatory reporters are required by law to report any cases of suspected child abuse. In most cases, the Department of Social Services is the lead investigative agency. In most states, social services are charged with investigating the report within 24 working hours of their notification. If social services conclude that the alleged abuse is supported by evidence, then they are charged with correcting the problem.

One of the most immediate modes for correcting the problem is the removal of the child from the home. However, removing a child from his/her home is usually the last resort. In most cases, the department of social services will attempt to work with the family to ensure that members of the family stay together. In some cases, depending upon the severity of the suspected abuse, the child is removed from the home and placed in emergency protective custody (EPC).

In most states, social services do not have the authority to act alone in placing a child into protective custody. For protective custody, a court order and law enforcement personnel are required to remove a child from his/her home.

Emergency Protective Custody

If a law enforcement officer is called to a home in which he/she feels that a child is in imminent danger, then that officer has the option of removing the child from the home and placing the child in emergency protective custody. If a social services agent, through the investigation of a report, deems it necessary for the protection of the child, he/she may also ask a law enforcement officer to take the child into emergency protective custody. In these instances, the child is removed from the home and, in most cases, placed with another family member who resides in another location or with a temporary foster family. The child remains separated from his/her residential family until the probable cause hearing.

Probable Cause Hearing

The purpose of a probable cause hearing is to determine if other reasonable efforts may be taken to protect the child from abuse in lieu of removing the child from the home. If the child was placed in a foster home because of EPC, this hearing is mandatory and, in many states, is known as the 72-hour hearing. If the child was placed with relatives during EPC, then generally this hearing is at the request of the parents who desire the return of their child.

During the probable cause hearing, the family court judge may decide to return the child to his/her parents or allow the child to remain in EPC until the removal or merits hearing. The merits hearing is generally held within 30–40 days of the date of EPC.

Merits Hearing

During the merits hearing, the parent or parents who have had their child or children removed through EPC now have the opportunity to "earn" the right to have their child(ren) returned to their custody. It is at this time that the parents are given a placement or treatment plan that may involve anger management therapy, counseling, or parenting classes. The parents are also given a date for their next hearing, a permanency planning hearing that will determine if appropriate measures are being taken to provide a better environment for the child. It is during this hearing that parents are informed of their cost in terms of child support and their visitation rights while the child is in temporary care.

Permanency Planning Hearing

If the parents have satisfied the requirements made at the merits hearing, then their child is returned to his/her home after the permanency planning hearing. If the parents have failed to satisfy the requirement of Social Services, then the permanency planning hearing is utilized to locate temporary placement of the child for up to one year. At the end of that period, Social Services has the option of returning the child to the home, continuing with temporary placement, or initiating permanent placement and the termination of parental rights.

Termination of Parental Rights

The process of the termination of parental rights is utilized if it is unlikely that a child can be returned to the custody of his/her parents. In this case, and depending upon the age of the child, the child may be placed in the custody of permanent foster parents, adoptive parents, or allowed to live independently of the parents. In removing a child from an abusive home, the goal is to protect the child. With legal strategies and laws (some in existence for nearly three decades), states and the federal government have attempted to ensure the right of safety to children.

Efforts Supporting the Protection of Children

It was nearly one century after the abuse and neglect of Mary Ellen Wilson in 1874 that federal and state efforts in the United States began to address the issues of child abuse. In 1972, the National Center for the Prevention of Child Abuse and Neglect was established to educate researchers and train public officials to recognize and prevent child abuse (Helfer & Kempe, 1987).

In 1974, the Child Abuse Prevention and Treatment Act was passed, which not only defined child abuse for the first time but also brought to the public's attention the suffering of children at the hands of adults (Crosson-Tower, 1999).

In 1984, the Child Protection Act addressed the topic of child pornography and the need for legal penalties for those who engage in the production and distribution of child pornography (McCabe & Lee, 1997).

In 1989, the General Assembly of the United Nations formulated the Declaration of the Rights of the Child, which concluded that a child, because of his/her physical and mental immaturity, requires safeguards and care (Crosson-Tower, 1999).

In 1994, under the Violent Crime Control and Law Enforcement Act (Title XVII), crimes against children were addressed to include sex offender registries and assaults against children (Reid, 1995).

In 1996, the Telecommunication Reform Act and the Child Pornography Protection Act were attempts to regulate information dispersed over the Internet to include child pornography (McCabe, 2000). However, in 2002, the U.S. Supreme Court decided to strike down a federal ban on "virtual" child pornography or the use of computer-generated child pornography.

Most of the recent legal efforts toward the prevention of child abuse have been supported by law enforcement and the community. Today people are not only interested in ending child abuse but also learning more about the cases of abused children. For a list of suggested popular books based upon cases of child abuse and neglect, see Appendix A.

Abuse Prevention Efforts

Today, there exist many strategies and programs to reduce the incidents of child abuse and neglect; however, most of the efforts fall into one of the following three categories: primary prevention, secondary prevention, and tertiary prevention (Crosson-Tower, 2002).

Primary prevention efforts attempt to address the underlying causes of child abuse such as poverty or inappropriate discipline, while secondary prevention efforts target those individuals at risk for abuse (Crosson-Tower, 2002). Tertiary prevention takes another approach in a retrospective research design and targets those individuals who have already been abused in an attempt to prevent repeat victimization (Orbach & Lamb, 1999).

Two of the more common tertiary prevention efforts to address child abuse are *Trauma-Specific Therapy* and the *Self-Trauma Model*. Both of these efforts are attempts to address a history of child abuse.

Trauma-Specific Therapy is most often applied in cases of child physical abuse and is based upon the assumptions that: (1) the abuse experience had specific negative psychosocial effects, and (2) treatment is enhanced when abuse outcomes are linked with a history of abuse (Berliner, 1997). For example, young women who are sexually promiscuous may address their behavior by understanding that adult sexual behavior is often a consequence of childhood sexual abuse. For many victims of sexual abuse, it was only through sex that they received attention as a child; hence they continue the behavior as an adult.

Self-Trauma Model is based upon three components: (1) identity (2) boundary, and (3) affect regulation. Specifically, identity addresses one's self-image; boundary addresses an awareness of the self and others, and affect regulation encompasses the ability to engage in internal activities to reduce negative affective states (Briere, 1997). For example, young adults may come to realize that not only do they have self-worth and that they are not responsible for the actions of others but also that there are mental exercises or practices that enable them to "de-stress" in circumstances of conflict or confrontation. Through the control of their affects, they begin to address their feelings of guilt, blame, and worthlessness.

Some of the programs implemented today in an attempt to reduce child abuse include life skills training in an effort to reduce financial stresses and to increase anger management abilities. Self-protection training programs also exist to inform and educate individuals on their risk for victimization. In addition, educational services programs inform the public on the subject of child abuse and neglect as well as help programs for at-risk families. Finally, law enforcement and social services programs target educators, film developers, and church leaders to inform these mandatory reporters on the signs of child abuse and neglect and their avenues for reporting possible cases of child victimization. These programs not only facilitate the reporting of abuse but also provide individuals with information on risk factors for and other sources of information on child abuse (Davies & Garwood, 2001).

Other attempts by states to reduce child abuse and neglect include the establishment of central registries on cases of child abuse and neglect to not only document the report of the case but also document its history. Also, stricter law enforcement policies on arrest in cases of child abuse and domestic violence have been implemented in an attempt to reduce the cases of child abuse as it is felt, by some researchers and practioners, that mandatory arrest policies significantly reduce subsequent attacks (Maxwell, Garner & Fagan, 2001). Finally, some states such as California have developed and implemented specific programs targeted toward certain aspects of child abuse. California, for example, has implemented a "Safe Arms" program to give young mothers who may be inclined to kill or abandon their newborn children a place to take the child (McManis, 2002). Participating hospitals will provide mothers a place to leave their newborns without fear of prosecution for abandoning their babies.

Some of the more recent law enforcement efforts to prevent child abuse include the Internet Crimes Against Children, State Sex Offender Registries, and the America's Missing Broadcasting Emergency Response (AMBER) Plan.

Internet Crimes Against Children

During 1998, the U.S. Department of Justice and the Office of Juvenile Justice and Delinquency Prevention (OJJDP) awarded 10 state and local law enforcement agencies across the country the funds to design and implement a program to counter the emerging issue of child pornography and the sexual exploitation of children via the Internet. These law enforcement agencies became members of the Internet Crimes Against Children (ICAC) Task Force Program.

Under this program, the law enforcement agencies serve as regional resources in the education and prevention of child sexual abuse via the Internet. In addition, it is the goal of these funded agencies to identify and investigate possible cases of the sexual abuse of children. In 2000, after a perceived "successful" two years of law enforcement efforts toward the identification of cases, OJJDP made 20 new awards to law enforcement agencies across the nation, bringing the ICAC Task Force Program to a total of 30 law enforcement agencies.

State Sex Offender Registries

In March of 1998, the Bureau of Justice Statistics (BJS) established the National Sex Offender Registry Assistance Program (NSOR-AP) to assist states in meeting the requirements of the Wetterling Act, as amended by Megan's Law, in terms of establishing a national convicted sex offender registry. As a result of NSOR-AP, approximately 390,000 convicted sex offenders were registered in 49 states and the District of Columbia during February of 2001 compared to approximately 275,000 registered in April of 1998. In addition, 22 states now include the collection of DNA samples as part of their registration process.

AMBER Plan

During the fall of 2001 the National Center for Missing and Exploited Children (NCMEC) began the AMBER Plan. Fueling the need for the AMBER plan are the statistics that approximately 4,500 non-family abductions are reported to law enforcement on an annual basis, that over 60% of these abductions involve a sexual assault, and that approximately 75% of the children murdered by a non-family member are killed within three hours of their abductions. The goal of the AMBER plan is to assist cities and towns across the United States in creating their own emergency alert plans for locating missing children.

The AMBER, created in 1996 after the abduction and brutal murder of Amber Hagerman in Arlington, Texas, is based upon three criteria: (1) a law-enforcement confirmed case of child abduction (2) a law-enforcement belief in the abducted child's danger of bodily harm, and (3) descriptive information on the child, the child's abductor, or the abductor's vehicle. If these criteria are met, then information is gathered and distributed to the public through radio and television stations within the area or throughout the country. As of the summer of 2002, the AMBER plan has been credited with recovering approximately 40 children. For other sources of information on child abuse and neglect, see Appendix B.

Factors for At-Risk Children

Specific indicators have been identified throughout this text for the four types of child abuse. In general, there are four overwhelming factors related to at-risk children: lack of attachment, substance abuse in the home, children who witness domestic violence, and children with special needs (Crosson-Tower, 2002).

Attachment or social attachment is related to the notion of social tie or bond among family members. Specifically, in

the case of child abuse, attachment refers to the relationship between parent and child. Children who have failed to
obtain or maintain that bond with their parent or parents
are at risk for not only abuse by the parent but also for
abuse by someone other than their parents. In particular, a
parent who fails to bond with his/her child places less importance on that child and his or her well-being. In addition,
a child who, because of minimal interactions and together-
ness with the parent, is perhaps starved for adult attention
and thus solicits that attention from other adults. Unfortunately, many adults who target children for abuse seek out
those attention-starved children.

Substance abuse in the home is another factor that
places a child at risk for abuse. Specifically, parents who
abuse substances are more likely to abuse their children or
to allow the abuse of their children by others. In addition, in
homes where substance abuse exists, the likelihood of the
child utilizing drugs or alcohol is increased; thus, the child
himself/herself is more likely to take part in abusive activities (Barkan, 2001).

Domestic violence in the home not only affects the adults
who are victimized but also the children who witness the
victimization. In many cases, children who witness domestic violence also become victims of domestic violence. Later
in life, in many cases, child victims of domestic violence or
those who witness domestic violence become either adult
perpetrators of domestic violence or adult victims of domestic violence (Hagemann-White, 2001; Kapur, 2001).

Finally, one cannot discount the impact of a special
needs child in the child abuse and neglect scenario. Children with disabilities require extra time and attention. In a
stressful home environment, the risk for child abuse is increased; adding to that stress the additional elements of a
special needs child puts the child then at an even greater
risk for victimization. For case studies and current statistics
on child abuse, see Appendix C.

Conclusion

Child abuse and neglect is concern for all nations. In the United States, children are victimized on a daily basis. Unfortunately for those children and in conflict with the concept of "stranger danger" most of the perpetrators of violence against children are the parents or caretakers of those children.

Whether the abuse is neglect, sexual, physical, or emotional, the child victims deserve not only to be protected from those abusers but given the opportunity to grow and develop in a loving and nurturing environment, whether that environment comes from the parents or society itself. A child today is an adult tomorrow. Only by protecting these children of today may we, as a society, protect our children of tomorrow.

Appendix A

Suggested Mass-Market Books Based upon Cases of Child Abuse and Neglect

Allison, D. (1992). *Bastard Out of Carolina*. New York, NY: Dutton.
Berry, J. (1992). *Lead Us Not into Temptation*. New York, NY: Doubleday.
Boyle, P. (1994). *Scout's Honor: Sexual Abuse in America's Most Trusted Institution*. Rocklin, CA: Prima.
Brady, K. (1979). *Father's Day*. New York, NY: Dell Books.
Butterfield, F. (1995). *All God's Children*. New York, NY: Avon Books.
Chase, T. (1987). *When Rabbits Howl*. New York, NY: Jove Books.
Crawford, C. (1979). *Mommie Dearest*. New York, NY: Berkley Books.
Dorris, M. (1989). *The Broken Cord*. New York, NY: HarperRow.
Eglinton, J. (1965). *Greek Love*. New York, NY: Oliver Layton.

Fraser, S. (1988). *My Father's House*. New York, NY: Ticknor and Fields.

Kellerman, J. (1993). *The Devil's Waltz*. New York, NY: Bantam.

Pelzer, D. (1995). *A Child Called It*. Edison, NJ: Health Communications, Inc.

Sanders, L. (1982). *The Case of Lucy Bending*. New York, NY: Berkley Books.

Sereny, G. (1998). *Cries Unheard. Why Children Kill: The Story of Mary Bell*. New York, NY: Henry Holt and Company.

Appendix B

Information Sources on Child Abuse and Neglect

American Humane Association
Dept 8827
Denver, CO 80263
Phone: 866-AHA-1877
www.americanhumane.org

American Professional Society on the Abuse of Children
940 N. E. 13th Street
CHO 3B-3406
Oklahoma City, OK 73104

Phone: 405–271–8202
www.apsac.org

Association to Benefit Children
419 East 86th Street
New York, NY 10028
Phone: 212–831–1322
www.a-b-c.org

Child Abuse Prevention Foundation
9440 Ruffin Court, Suite 2
San Diego, CA 92123
Phone: 858–278–4400
www.capc-coco.org

Children's Bureau
330 C. St., SW, Room 2068
Washington, DC 20201
Phone: 202–205–8618
www.acf.dhhs.gov/programs/cb/

Child Welfare League of America
440 First Street NW, 3rd Floor
Washington, DC 20001
Phone: 202–638–2952
www.cwla.org

Disability, Abuse, and Personal Rights Project
P.O. Box T
Culver City, CA 90230
Phone: 310–391–2420
www.disability-abuse.com

Head Start Bureau
330 C. St., SW, Room 2018
Washington, DC 20201
Phone: 202–205–8572
www.acf.dhhs.gov/programs/hsb/

Kempe Children's Center
1825 Marion Street
Denver, CO 80218
Phone: 303-864-5254
www.kempecenter.org

National Alliance of Children's Trust and Prevention Funds
1730 K Street, Suite 304
Washington, DC 20006
Phone: 202-296-6645
www.msu.edu/user/millsda/

National Association of Counsel for Children
1825 Marion Street, Suite 340
Denver, CO 80218
Phone: 888-828-NACC
www.naccchildlaw.org

National Center for Missing and Exploited Children
699 Prince Street
Alexandria, VA 22314
Phone: 800-the-lost
www.missingkids.org

National Clearinghouse on Child Abuse and Neglect
Information
330 C. Street SW
Washington, DC 20447
Phone: 800-394-3366
www.calib.com

National Committee to Prevent Child Abuse
2950 Tennyson Street
Denver, CO 80212
Phone: 877-224-8233
www.childabuse.org

National Criminal Justice Reference Service (NCJRS) Office
of Justice Programs
810 Seventh Street SW
Washington, DC 20531
Phone: 202-307-5933
www.ncjrs.org

National Data Archive on Child Abuse and Neglect
College of Human Ecology
Cornell University
Ithaca, NY 14853
Phone: 607-255-7799
www.ndacan.cornell.edu

National Exchange Club Foundation
3050 Central Avenue
Toledo, OH 43606
Phone: 800-924-2643
www.preventchildabuse.com

National Indian Child Welfare Association
5100 S.W. Macadam Avenue, Suite 300
Portland, OR 97239
Phone: 503-222-4044
www.nicwa.org

Prevent Child Abuse America
200 S. Michigan Avenue, 17th Floor
Chicago, IL 60604
Phone: 312-663-3520
www.preventchildabuse.org

The Natural Child Project
P.O. Box 3183
Sunriver, OR 97709
Phone: 866-593-1547
www.naturalchild.org

Appendix C

Tommy: A Case of Physical Abuse

Tommy was 4 years old when he received his first punch from his father; that particular punch left him breathless and with two broken ribs. Although his mother lived in the home with Tommy, his three other siblings, and his father, she never intervened to help him when his father was punishing him. On several occasions after that incident, especially when his father was drinking alcohol on a regular basis, Tommy was cut, burned with a cigarette, and tied to a steam radiator as punishments for various actions. Tommy ran away from home at age 11 and survived on the street by stealing and selling drugs until his arrest at age 13. After his first arrest he was placed in a juvenile detention center for six months, then released to the custody of his father. Two weeks later the physical abuse at home resumed and he ran away again, for the final time. By the time Tommy reached the age of 18, he had been in and out of the detention center three additional times. After meeting and marrying Crystal, he was arrested for domestic violence at the age of 20.

The physical abuse of children includes cases of injuries such as bruises, welts, burns, lacerations, bone fractures, and other evidence of physical injury. According to the U.S. Department of Justice and the Office of Justice Programs in 2001, the ages of child victims of physical abuse varied, with the majority of the reported victims of age 12 or older. However, physically abused children who begin participating in criminal activity (as compared to non-abused children) are generally younger at the time of their first arrest, commit nearly twice as many offenses, and are arrested more frequently. The following table displays the age distribution for reported victims of child physical abuse during 2001.

Child Physical Abuse Victims by Age (2001)

Age	Percent
0–3	11%
4–7	13%
8–11	15%
12–15	37%
16–17	24%

Source: U.S. Department of Justice. Office of Justice Programs. Office of Juvenile Justice and Delinquency Prevention. Child Abuse Reported to the Police. *Juvenile Justice Bulletin* (May, 2001).

Jenny: A Case of Sexual Abuse

Jenny was 13 when her mother left her, her father, and her two brothers, James (age 17) and Charlie (age 7). As she was the only female in the house, she began doing all of the cooking, cleaning, and laundry for "her men." Her father, a self-proclaimed "religious man" and leader of the church youth group, enforced the notion of a woman's place in the home and expected her to not only "keep house" for him but also prepare snacks every Sunday night for the church youth meetings. Jenny, although she excelled in the care of her family, began falling behind in her schoolwork. One evening, after she had washed the dinner dishes and was preparing for bed, Jenny was approached by her father for sex. As she had for months felt as though she was the "mother" of the family, she agreed to begin having sexual intercourse with her father, as she would now be the "wife." Her father confessed his love for her and, at 14, she loved him. Jenny and her father continued their incestuous relationship until Jenny was 17. At 17 Jenny met Ben, a young man in her class. As Jenny was now three grade levels behind most of the other students in her class, she was often the subject of "dumb blonde" jokes; however, Ben did not tease her; in fact, Ben showed her attention. As might have been anticipated, Ben's interest in Jenny was not welcomed by her father. As Jenny began dating Ben, her father began to ignore his daughter and no longer expressed interest in her as a sexual partner or as a daughter. When Jenny became pregnant with Ben's child, her father kicked her out of the home. Ben, who was not interested in becoming a father, began dating another classmate. Jenny's baby girl now lives with her older brother James and his wife. Jenny has since been arrested multiple times for prostitution and for attempting to purchase illegal drugs. Her family has not seen or heard from her in years. Today is Jenny's birthday. If she is alive, she is 24.

The sexual abuse of children varies from a relatively nonspecific charge of assault and battery with intent to gratify sexual desires to more specific charges such as fondling, sodomy, rape, and incest. According to the 2001 statistics of the U.S. Department of Justice and the Office of Justice Programs, the ages of child victims of sexual abuse varied.

However, 13% of those victims were between birth and age 3. Given the fact that in many cases of child sexual abuse there are no physical signs of abuse, and the fact that children under the age of four lack the verbal skills necessary to report abuse, it is suggested that the actual proportion of very young victims is much higher. The following table displays the age distributions of reported child sexual abuse victims for 2001.

Child Sexual Abuse Victims by Age (2001)

Age	Percent
0–3	13%
4–7	27%
8–11	22%
12–15	29%
16–17	9%

Source: U.S. Department of Justice. Office of Justice Programs. Office of Juvenile Justice and Delinquency Prevention. Child Abuse Reported to the Police. *Juvenile Justice Bulletin* (May, 2001).

Sarah: A Case of Emotional Abuse

As far back as she can remember Sarah has known that her mother disliked her. Perhaps the reasoning behind the dislike was the fact that Sarah looked like her father (the man that cheated and left her mother) or the fact that her paternal grandparents often insisted upon unannounced visits with the granddaughter and gifts for her despite Sarah's mother's protests. When Sarah was small and discovered that she liked peanut butter and jelly sandwiches, her mother commented on her weight gain and told her that the sandwiches were making her fat. When she became older and wanted to go to college, her mother dismissed the idea not because the costs were out of reach but because Sarah was "too dumb" for college. When she did go to college (with her grandparents' support) and complete her baccalaureate degree, her mother's remark was that "money could buy anything." Sarah experienced years of unsuccessful dating relationships (some of which were verbally abusive), and as each relationship deteriorated, Sarah's mother always proclaimed the broken relationship as Sarah's fault. At the age of 23, Sarah committed suicide.

Jeremy and Michael: A Case of Neglect

Jeremy, a 7-year-old boy, was found by law enforcement officers at home in his unheated trailer on a winter day dressed only in a pair of lightweight pants and a short-sleeved shirt. Jeremy was taking care of his 18-month-old brother Michael on that day. Michael had been left in his playpen dressed in only a shirt and dirty diaper with a bowl of dry cereal in the playpen. A box of cereal had been left on the kitchen counter for Jeremy. Their father was not involved in the lives of the boys, and their mother worked 8–10-hour shifts at a nearby convenience store. Neighbors, who had witnessed the mother leaving the boys on a daily basis while she worked and then again at night while she went out, had summoned law enforcement to the home. Jeremy was dirty; he was malnourished; he was not attending school, and his teeth were in need of attention. Michael was dirty, malnourished, and ill with an inner ear infection.

In all cases of child abuse, there exist elements of emotional abuse. In some cases of child abuse, there exists only emotional abuse. The emotional abuse may be in the form of belittling, rejecting, ignoring or terrorizing the child; however, most researchers in the area of child abuse view emotional abuse as the most damaging form of abuse over the long-term.

Cases of neglect reflect a judgment on childcare that is deemed unacceptable by the general public. These cases include the failure to properly feed, clothe, or shelter children as well as a failure to seek medical attention and education for the child. It has been suggested by the Department of Justice, that approximately 20% of those individuals arrested for crimes of violence had been victims of neglect.

Data from the U.S. Department of Justice and the Office of Justice Programs in 1997 suggest that there does appear to exist a relationship between the prevalence of child abuse and various negative outcomes of violence, pregnancy, drug use, lower grade point average (GPA), and mental health problems during adolescence. The following table displays some of those outcomes.

Negative Life Outcomes of Abused Versus Non-Abused Children (1997)

Outcome	Abused (%)	Non-Abused (%)
Violence	70	56
Pregnancy	52	34
Drug Use	43	32
Lower GPA	33	23
Mental Health Problems	26	15

Source: U.S. Department of Justice. Office of Justice Programs. Office of Juvenile Justice and Delinquency Prevention. In the Wake of Childhood Maltreatment. *Juvenile Justice Bulletin* (August 1997).

As released by the U.S. Department of Health and Human Services and the Administration for Children and Families in 2001, the victimization rate of children in this country has fluctuated over the last decade, with an average rate of 13.9 child victims per 1,000 children. The following table displays the child victimization rates for the United States by year.

Child Victimization Rates (1990—2000)

Year	Rate	Year	Rate
2000	12.2	1994	15.2
1999	11.8	1993	15.3
1998	12.9	1992	15.1
1997	13.8	1991	14.0
1996	14.7	1990	13.
1995	14.7		

Source: U.S. Department of Health. The Administration for Children and Families. Children's Bureau. *Factsheet Publications*, 2000.

In regard to the types of child abuse, the U.S. Department of Health and Human Services and the Administration for Children and Families note that from 1996 to 2000 the rates (per 1,000 children) of physical abuse have decreased, the rates of neglect have fluctuated, the rates of sexual abuse have decreased, and the rates of emotional abuse have fluctuated. The following table displays those reported rates of child abuse for the United States by year.

Childhood Maltreatment by Type of Abuse (1996—2000)

Year	Physical Abuse	Neglect	Sexual Abuse	Emotional Abuse
2000	2.3	7.3	1.2	2.7
1999	2.5	6.5	1.3	4.4
1998	2.9	6.9	1.5	4.1
1997	3.3	7.5	1.7	1.8
1996	3.5	7.6	1.8	2.9

Source: U.S. Department of Health. The Administration for Children and Families. Children's Bureau. *Factsheet Publications*, 2000.

In regard to the youngest victims of child abuse (age 0–3), it was reported by the U.S. Department of Health and Human Services and the Administration for Children and Families in 2001 that the victimization rates (per 1,000 children) varied by the 48 states reporting. Specifically, the states of Alaska, Florida, Maine, Massachusetts, and North Carolina reported the highest rates of young (age 0–3) child victimizations whereas Missouri, New Hampshire, New Jersey, Pennsylvania, and Virginia reported the lowest rates of victimization. The following table displays the rates (per 1,000 children) of victimization for children age 0–3.

Of the estimated 3 million cases referred to Child Protective Services, during 2000, approximately 60% were investigated or assessed for merit. Approximately 30% of those cases investigated or assessed were substantiated. In many instances (as is too often the case), an additional incident or incidents were reported within six months of the first report. Specifically, as displayed in the table below,

Child Victimization Rates (2000) by State

State	Rate	State	Rate	State	Rate
Alabama	10.5	Kentucky	23.7	Ohio	23.8
Alaska	47.0	Louisiana	11.0	Oklahoma	22.9
Arizona	8.4	Maine	24.2	Oregon	22.7
Arkansas	11.2	Massachusetts	25.8	Pennsylvania	1.5
California	17.5	Michigan	14.6	Rhode Island	18.5
Colorado	9.1	Minnesota	8.5	South Carolina	13.8
Connecticut	22.0	Mississippi	9.6	South Dakota	14.4
Delaware	11.2	Missouri	6.0	Tennessee	15.4
Florida	35.6	Montana	21.8	Texas	10.5
Georgia	16.9	Nebraska	11.5	Utah	14.0
Hawaii	17.7	Nevada	16.9	Vermont	8.2
Idaho	11.0	New Hampshire	3.2	Virginia	5.6
Illinois	15.5	New Jersey	6.2	Washington	7.3
Indiana	15.9	New Mexico	14.1	West Virginia	22.8
Iowa	22.1	New York	19.3	Wisconsin	8.4
Kansas	14.5	North Carolina	24.7	Wyoming	15.1

Source: U.S. Department of Health. The Administration for Children and Families. Children's Bureau. *Factsheet Publications*, 2000.

Child Abuse: Recurrence of Cases (%) Within 6 Months of Initial Report.

State	Rate	State	Rate	State	Rate
Arizona	6.1	Kentucky	8.6	North Carolina	12.9
Arkansas	5.6	Louisiana	8.0	Oklahoma	8.5
California	10.7	Maine	4.7	Pennsylvania	11.7
Connecticut	11.4	Massachusetts	10.2	Rhode Island	3.5
Delaware	3.0	Michigan	3.3	South Dakota	12.4
Florida	6.7	Minnesota	4.6	Texas	4.2
Hawaii	6.4	Missouri	5.9	Utah	7.1
Illinois	9.7	Nebraska	8.1	Vermont	7.9
Indiana	8.2	New Hampshire	8.0	Washington	11.9
Iowa	11.8	New Jersey	5.8	West Virginia	6.7
Kansas	7.8	New York	8.5	Wyoming	6.8

Source: U.S. Department of Health. The Administration for Children and Families. Children's Bureau. *Factsheet Publications*, 2000.

Child Abuse: Recurrence of Cases (%) Within 6 Months of Initial Report

State	Rate	State	Rate	State	Rate
Alabama	10.5	Kansas	7.8	North Carolina	12.9
Arizona	6.1	Kentucky	8.6	Oklahoma	8.5
Arkansas	5.6	Louisiana	8.0	Pennsylvania	11.7
California	10.7	Maine	4.7	Rhode Island	3.5
Connecticut	11.4	Massachusetts	10.2	South Dakota	12.4
Delaware	3.0	Michigan	3.3	Texas	4.2
Florida	6.7	Minnesota	4.6	Utah	7.1
Hawaii	6.4	Missouri	5.9	Vermont	7.9
Illinois	9.7	Nebraska	8.1	Washington	11.9
Indiana	8.2	New Hampshire	8.0	West Virginia	6.7
Iowa	11.8	New Jersey	5.8	Wyoming	6.8
		New York	8.5		

Source: U.S. Department of Health. The Administration for Children and Families. Children's Bureau. *Factsheet Publications,* 2000.

and as reported in 2001 by the U.S. Department of Justice and the Administration for Children and Families, in the 33 reporting states, approximately 10% of the children were victims of recurrent abuse within six months of the initial report.

The 1997 Survey of Inmates in State Correctional Facilities, produced by the U.S. Department of Justice, the Bu-

Prisoner Characteristics of Violent Offenders (Child vs. Adult Victims), 1997

Characteristic	Offenders Against Children	Offenders Against Adults
Crime	Sex Offenses (65%)	Violent Non-Sex Offenses
(93%)		
Race	White (64%)	White (41%)
Age at Arrest	31+ (51%)	31+ (34%)
Marital Status	Ever Married (56%)	Ever Married (40%)
Relation to Victim	Relative/Intimate (48%)	Stranger (54%)
	Acquaintance (38%)	
Weapon	No Weapon (82%)	No Weapon (49%)

Source: U.S. Department of Justice. Office of Justice Programs. Office of Juvenile Justice and Delinquency Prevention. Offenders Incarcerated for Crimes Against Juveniles. *Juvenile Justice Bulletin* (December, 2001).

reau of Justice Statistics, and the Federal Bureau of Prisons
suggests that offenders against children differ from offenders against adults. Specifically, as displayed in the table at
the bottom of page 101, they differ in crime, race, age, marital status, relation to victim, and weapon used.

References

Chapter 1

Bartollas, C. (2000). *Juvenile Delinquency* (5th ed.). Boston, MA: Allyn and Bacon.

Brownstein, H. H. (2000). *The Social Reality of Violence and Violent Crime*. Boston, MA: Allyn and Bacon.

Chesser, E. (1952). *Cruelty to Children*. New York, NY: Philosophical Library.

Crosson-Tower, C. (1999). *Understanding Child Abuse and Neglect* (4th ed.). Boston, MA: Allyn and Bacon.

Damme, C. (1978). The Worth of an Infant Under Law. *Medical History, 22*(1), 1–24.

DeShaney v. Winnebago County Department of Social Services, 109 S. Ct. 98 (1989).

Finkelhor, D. & Ormrod, R. (2001). *Child Abuse Reported to the Police.*

Washington, DC: U.S. Department of Justice. Office of Justice Programs. Office of Juvenile Justice and Delinquency Prevention, Washington, DC (NCJ-187238).

Garbarino, J., Guttman, E. & Seeley, J. W. (1986). *The Psychologically Battered Child.* San Francisco, CA: Jossey-Bass.

Kelley, B. T., Thornberry, T. P., & Smith, C. A. (1997). *In the Wake of Childhood Maltreatment.* Washington, DC: U.S. Department of Justice. Office of Justice Programs. Office of Juvenile Justice and Delinquency Prevention (NCJ-165257).

Langstaff, J. & Sleeper, T. (2001). *The National Center on Child Fatality Review.* Washington, DC: U.S. Department of Justice. Office of Justice Programs. Office of Juvenile Justice and Delinquency Prevention (FS-200112).

Malinowski, B. (1927). *Sex and Repression in Savage Society.* London: Routledge and Kegan Paul.

Martin, H. P. (1972). The Child and His Development. In C. Kempe and R. E. Helfer (eds.) *Helping the Battered Child and His Family.* Philadelphia, PA: J. B. Lippincott, pp. 93–114.

McCabe, K. A. (2000). Child Pornography and the Internet. *Social Science Computer Review, 18*(1), 73–76.

Morgan, L. H. (1877). *Ancient Society.* Chicago, IL: Kerr.

O'Driscoll, P. (1999). Case Was Botched Start-to-Finish. Some Say JonBenet Jury Seen as Police Failure. *USA Today,* 3A, October 14.

Radbill, S. X. (1987). A History of Child Abuse. In R. E. Helfer and R. S. Kempe (eds.) *The Battered Child* (4th ed.). Chicago, IL: University of Chicago Press.

Riis, J. (1892). *The Children of the Poor.* London: Sampson, Low, & Marston.

Sanger, W. W. (1898). *History of Prostitution.* New York, NY: Medical Publishing.

Sedlak, A. J. & Broadhurst, D. D. (1996). *Executive Summary of the Third National Incidence Study of Child Abuse and Neglect. National Clearinghouse on Child Abuse and Neglect Information.* Washington, DC: U.S. Department of Health and Human Services. The Administration for Children and Families. National Center on Child Abuse and Neglect (ACF-1059418).

Sorel, N. C. (1984). *Ever Since Eve: Personal Reflections on Childbirth.* New York, NY: Oxford University Press.

Stadum, B. (1995). The Dilemma in Saving Children from Child Labor: Reform and Casework at Odds with Family Needs (1900–1938). *Child Welfare, 74*(1), 33–55.

Thomas, M. P. (1972). Child Abuse and Neglect, Part I: Historical Overview, Legal Material and Social Perspective. *North Carolina Law Review, 50,* 293-349.

Unnithan, P. (1994). The Processing of Homicide Cases with Child Victims: Systematic and Situational Contingencies. *Journal of Criminal Justice, 22*(1), 41–50.

Wallace, H. (1999). *Family Violence. Legal, Medical, and Social Perspectives* (2nd ed.). Boston, MA: Allyn and Bacon.

Wilson, J. (2000). *1999 Report Series. Children as Victims.* U.S. Department of Justice. Office of Justice Programs. Office of Juvenile Justice and Delinquency Prevention (NCJ-180753164).

Chapter 2

Aber, J. L. & Allen, J. P. (1987). Effects of Maltreatment on Young Children's Socio-Emotional Development: An Attachment Theory Perspective. *Developmental Psychology, 23*(3), 406–414.

Ainsworth, M. D. S., Blehar, M., Waters, E. & Wall, S. (1978). *Patterns of Attachment.* Hillsdale, NJ: Lawrence Erlbaum.

Artingstall, K. A. (1995). Munchausen Syndrome by Proxy. *FBI Law Enforcement Bulletin,* 5–11, August.

Barkan, S. E. (2001). *Criminology. A Sociological Understanding* (2nd ed.). Upper Saddle River, NJ: Prentice Hall.

Bartollas, C. (2000). *Juvenile Delinquency* (5th ed.). Boston, MA: Allyn and Bacon.

Bottoms, B. L. & Davis, S. L. (1997). The Creation of Satanic Ritual Abuse. *Journal of Social and Clinical Psychology, 16*(2), 112–132.

Bottoms, B. L., Shaver, P. R., & Goodman, G. S. (1996). An Analysis of Ritualistic and Religion-Related Child Abuse Allegations. *Law and Human Behavior, 20*(1), 1–34.

Bynum, J. E. & Thompson, W. E. (2002). *Juvenile Delinquency: A Sociological Approach* (5th ed.). Boston, MA: Allyn and Bacon.

Crosson-Tower, C. (1999). *Understanding Child Abuse and Neglect* (4th ed.) Boston, MA: Allyn and Bacon.

Davis, J. (1982). *Help Me, I'm Hurt.* Dubuque, IA: Kendall Hunt.

Faller, K. & Ziefert, M. (1981). Causes of Child Abuse and Neglect. In K. Faller (ed.) *Social Work with Abused and Neglected Children.* New York, NY: Free Press.

Federal Bureau of Investigation (1997). *National Incident-Based Reporting System (NIBRS).* 12 states only. Computer file. Tabulations undertaken by Crimes Against Children Research Center, Washington, DC: U.S. Department of Justice. Federal Bureau of Investigation.

Finkelhor, D. & Ormrod, R. (2001). *Child Abuse Reported to the Police.* Washington, DC: U.S. Department of Justice. Office of Justice Programs. Office of Juvenile Justice and Delinquency Prevention, Washington, DC (NCJ-187238).

Gelles, R. (1973). Child Abuse as Psychopathology: A Sociological Critique and Reformation. *American Journal of Orthopsychiatry, 43,* 611–621.

Gil, D. (1970). *Violence Against Children.* Cambridge, MA: Harvard University Press.

Goldstein, R. D. (1999). *Child Abuse and Neglect: Cases and Materials.* St. Paul, MN: West.

Jackson, S., Thompson, R. A., Christiansen, E. H., Colman, R. A., Wyatt, J., Buckendahl, C. W., Wilcox, B. L., & Peterson, R. (1999). Predicting Abuse-prone Parental Attitudes and Discipline Practices in a Nationally Representative Sample. *Child Abuse, 23*(1), 15–19.

Kelley, T. (2001). Metro Briefing New York: The Bronx Mother Charged in Child's Death. *New York Times,* D8, December 19.

Martin, H. P. (1972). The Child and His Development. In C. Kempe and R. E. Helfer (eds.) *Helping the Battered Child and His Family.* Philadelphia, PA: J. B. Lippincott, pp. 93–114.

Martin, H. P. & Beezley, P. (1976). Personality of Abused Children. In H. P. Martin (ed.) *The Abused Child.* Cambridge, MA: Ballinger, pp. 105–111.

McNeese, M. C. & Hebeler, J. R. (1977). The Abused Child: A Clinical Approach to Identification and Management. *Clinical Symposia, 29*(5), 1–36.

Milner, J. S. & Dopke, C. (1997). Child Physical Abuse. Review of Offender Characteristics. In D. A. Wolfe and K. J McMahan (eds.) *Child Abuse: New Directions in Prevention and Treatment Across the Lifespan.* Thousand Oaks, CA: Sage.

Neubauer, D. W. (1991). *Judicial Process: Law, Court, and Politics in the United States.* Pacific Grove, CA: Brooks/Cole.

Ounsted, C., Oppenheimer, R., & Lindsay, J. (1974). Aspects of Bonding Failure: The Psychopathology and Psychotherapeutic Treatment of Families and Battered Children. *Developmental Medicine and Child and Neurology, 16*(2), 447–452.

Pressel, D. M. (2000). Evaluation of Physical Abuse in Children. *American Family Physician* (May 15, 2000). Available at http://www.aafp.org/afp/20000515/3057.html. Accessed January 17, 2001.

Reid, S. T. (1995). *Criminal Law* (3rd ed.). Upper Saddle River, NJ: Prentice Hall.

Rodeheffer, M. & Martin, H. P. (1976). Special Problems in the Developmental Assessment of Abused Children. In H. P. Martin (ed.) *The Abused Child.* Cambridge, MA: Ballinger, pp. 113-128.

Sedlak, A. J. & Broadhurst, D. D. (1996). *Executive Summary of the Third National Incidence Study of Child Abuse and Neglect. National Clearinghouse on Child Abuse and Neglect Information.* Washington,

DC: U.S. Department of Health and Human Services. The Administration for Children and Families. National Center on Child Abuse and Neglect (ACF-1059418).

Siegel, L. (2000). *Criminology* (7th ed.). Belmont, CA: Wadsworth.

Simon, R., Wu, C., Johnson, C. & Conger, R. (1995). A Test of Various Perspectives on the Intergenerational Transmission of Domestic Violence. *Criminology, 33*(1), 141–171.

Stanley, S. A. (2001). Man Charged with Shaking Child to Death: Toddler's Spinal Cord Snapped. *The Times Picayune* (New Orleans), B1, December 8.

State of North Carolina v. Sheree Vonelle Suddreth Byrd and Joseph Allen Byrd No. 159A83 309 N. C. 132; 305 S. E. 2d. 724; 1983 N. C. Lexis 1322.

State of Ohio v. Higgins, Appellant No. 88AP-633 61 Ohio App. 3d 414, 572 N. E. 2d 834; 1990 Ohio App. Lexis 1370.

State v. Thorpe, 429 A. 2d 785 (R.I. 1981).

Stone, F. B. (1989). Munchausen-by-Proxy: An Unusual Form of Child Abuse. *Social Casework, 70*(4), 243–246.

Wallace, H. (1999). *Family Violence. Legal, Medical, and Social Perspectives* (2nd ed.). Boston, MA: Allyn and Bacon.

Wiehe, V. R. (1997). *Sibling Abuse. Hidden Physical, Emotional, and Sexual Trauma* (2nd ed.). Thousand Oaks, CA: Sage.

Wolfgang, M. (1958). *Patterns of Criminal Homicide.* Philadelphia, PA: University of Pennsylvania Press.

Chapter 3

Abel, G. G. (1987). Self-Reported Sex Crimes of Non-Incarcerated Paraphiliacs. *Journal of Interpersonal Violence, 2*(1), 3–25.

Administration for Children and Families [ACF]. (1999). 1999 National Child Abuse and Neglect Reporting System. Highlights of Findings. Washington, DC: US Dept. of Health and Human Services. http://www.acf.dhhs.gov/programs/cb/publications/cm99/high.html accessed January 20, 2001.

Barkan, S. E. (2001). *Criminology. A Sociological Understanding* (2nd ed.). Upper Saddle River, NJ: Prentice Hall.

Bartollas, C. (2000). *Juvenile Delinquency* (5th ed.). Boston, MA: Allyn and Bacon.

Briere, J. N. & Elliott, D. M. (1994). Immediate and Long-term Impacts of Child Sexual Abuse. In R. E. Behrman *The Future of Children. Sexual Abuse of Children, 4*(2), 70–83.

Brown, A. & Finkelhor, D. (1986). Impact of Child Sexual Abuse: A Review of the Research. *Psychological Bulletin, 99*(1), 66–77.

Bynum, J. E. & Thompson, W. E. (2002). *Juvenile Delinquency A Sociological Approach* (5th ed.). Boston, MA: Allyn and Bacon.

Carroll, C. (2001). Preliminary Hearing Scheduled for Man Charged with Sexual Abuse of Foster Sons. Hillsboro Man Faces a Minimum of 5 Years in Prison. *St. Louis Post Dispatch,* A2 (December 31).

Clark, P. E. (1999). *An Evaluation of Child Sexual Abuse Cases in Lexington County, South Carolina.* University of South Carolina: College of Criminal Justice. Master's thesis.

Crosson-Tower, C. (1999). *Understanding Child Abuse and Neglect* (4th ed.). Boston, MA: Allyn and Bacon.

Crosson-Tower, C. (2002). *When Children are Abused. An Educator's Guide to Intervention.* Boston, MA: Allyn and Bacon.

DeYoung, M. (1982). *The Sexual Victimization of Children.* Jefferson, NC: McFarland.

Duncan, L. E. & Williams, L. M. (1998). Gender Role Socialization and Male-on-Male vs Female-on-Male Child Sexual Abuse. *Sex Roles, 39*(9/10), 765–785.

Faller, K. C. (1988). *Child Sexual Abuse.* New York, NY: Columbia University Press.

Federal Bureau of Investigation (1997). *National Incident-Based Reporting System (NIBRS).* 12 states only. Computer file. Tabulations Undertaken by Crimes Against Children Research Center, Washington, DC: U.S. Department of Justice. Federal Bureau of Investigation.

Finkelhor, D. (1984). *Child Sexual Abuse. New Theories and Research.* New York, NY: Free Press.

Finkelhor, D. & Ormrod, R. (2001). *Child Abuse Reported to the Police.* Washington, DC: U.S. Department of Justice. Office of Justice Programs. Office of Juvenile Justice and Delinquency Prevention, Washington, DC (NCJ-187238).

Furby, L., Weinrott, M. & Blackshaw, L. (1989). Sex Offender Recidivism: A Review. *Psychology Bulletin, 105*(1), 3–30.

Gebhard, P., Gagnon, J., Pomeroy, W. & Christenson, C. (1965). *Sex Offenders: An Analysis of Types.* New York, NY: Harper & Row.

Grimstad, H. & Schei, B. (1999). Pregnancy and Delivery for Women with a History of Child Sexual Abuse. *Child Abuse and Neglect, 23*(1), 81–90.

Gully, K. J., Britton, H., Hansen, K., Goodwin, K. & Nope, J. L. (1999). A New Measure for Distress During Child Sexual Abuse Examinations: The Genital Examination Distress Scale. *Child Abuse and Neglect, 23*(1), 61–70.

Helfer, R. E. & Kempe, R. S. (1987). *The Battered Child* (4th ed.). Chicago, IL: University of Chicago Press.

James, B. & Nasjleti, M. (1983). *Treating Sexually Abused Children and Their Families.* Palo Alto, CA: Consulting Psychologists Press.

Johnson, T. C. & Feldmeth, J. R. (1993). Sexual Behavior: A Continuum. In E. Gil & T. C. Johnson (eds.) *Sexualized Children and Children Who Molest*. Rockville, MD: Launch Press, pp. 41–52.

Kercher, G. A. & McShane, M. (1984). The Prevalence of Child Sexual Abuse Victimization in an Adult Sample of Texas Residents. *Child Abuse and Neglect, 8*(2), 495–501.

Lanning, K. (1992). *Child Sex Rings: A Behavioral Analysis for Criminal Justice Professionals Handling Cases of Child Sexual Exploitation* (3rd ed.). Quantico, VA: Federal Bureau of Investigation. Behavioral Science Unit.

Laviola, M. (1992). Effects of Older Brother-Younger Sister Incest: A Study of the Dynamics in 17 Cases. *Child Abuse and Neglect, 16*(3), 409–421.

Mayer, A. (1983). *Incest. A Treatment Manual for Therapy with Victims, Spouses, and Offenders*. Holmes Beach, FL: Learning Publications.

McCabe, K. A. (2000). Child Pornography and the Internet. *Social Science Computer Review, 18*(1), 73–76.

McCabe, K. A., & Gregory, S. S. (1997). *The Nature of South Carolina Violent Crime*. Columbia, SC: S.C. Dept. of Public Safety. Office of Safety and Grants.

Medaris, M. & Girouard, C. (2002). *Protecting Children in Cyberspace: The ICAC Task Force Program*. Washington, DC: U.S. Department of Justice. Office of Justice Programs. Office of Juvenile Justice and Delinquency Prevention. (NCJ-191213).

Mehta, M. & Plaza, D. (1997). Content Analysis of Pornographic Images Available on the Internet. *The Information Society, 13*(2), 153–162.

Office for Victims of Crime [OVC]. (2001). *Internet Crimes Against Children*. Washington, DC: U.S. Dept. of Justice. Office of Justice Programs.

Pollock, J. (1997). *Prisons Today and Tomorrow*. Gaithersburg, MD: Aspen.

Radbill, S. X. (1987). A History of Child Abuse. In R. E. Helfer and R. S. Kempe (eds.) *The Battered Child* (4th ed.). Chicago, IL: University of Chicago Press.

Rosenwald, M. (2002). Child Porn Purveyors Get Younger. The New Generation Taps Internet Power. *The Boston Globe*, B1, May 26.

Russell, D. (1983). The Incidents and Prevalence of Intrafamilial and Extrafamilial Sexual Abuse of Female Children. *Child Abuse and Neglect, 7*(1), 133–146.

Schremp, V. (2001). Man Gets Life in Abduction, Sex Assault of Girl, 9. *St. Louis Post Dispatch*, C2, December 11.

Sedlak, A. J. & Broadhurst, D. D. (1996). *Executive Summary of the Third National Incidence Study of Child Abuse and Neglect*. National

Clearinghouse on Child Abuse and Neglect Information. Washington, DC: U.S. Department of Health and Human Services. The Administration for Children and Families. National Center on Child Abuse and Neglect (ACF-1059418).

Sgroi, S. (1982). *Handbook of Clinical Intervention in Child Sexual Abuse.* Lexington, MA: Lexington Books.

Shane, S. (2002). State Restricts Lawsuits of Sexual Abuse Victims. Civil Claims Must be Filed Before Accuser Turns 21. *The Baltimore Sun,* A1, May 26.

Tsun, O. K. A. (1999). Sibling Incest: A Hong Kong Experience. *Child Abuse and Neglect, 23*(1), 71–80.

Wallace, H. (1999). *Family Violence. Legal, Medical, and Social Perspectives* (2nd ed.). Boston, MA: Allyn and Bacon.

Wiehe, V. R. (1997). *Sibling Abuse. Hidden Physical, Emotional, and Sexual Trauma* (2nd ed.). Thousand Oaks, CA: Sage.

Wyatt, G. E., Loeb, T. B., Solis, B. Carmona, J. V. & Romero, G. (1999). The Prevalence and Circumstances of Child Sexual Abuse: Changes Across a Decade. *Child Abuse and Neglect, 23*(1), 45–60.

Chapter 4

Barkan, S. E. (2001). *Criminology. A Sociological Understanding* (2nd ed.). Upper Saddle River, NJ: Prentice Hall.

Barongan, C. & Hall, G. C. N. (1995). The Influence of Misogynous Rap Music on Sexual Aggression Against Women, *Psychology of Women Quarterly, 19*(1), 195–207.

Bartollas, C. (2000). *Juvenile Delinquency* (5th ed.). Boston, MA: Allyn and Bacon.

Bynum, J. E. & Thompson, W. E. (2002). *Juvenile Delinquency A Sociological Approach* (5th ed.). Boston, MA: Allyn and Bacon.

Covitz, J. (1986). *Emotional Child Abuse: The Family Curse.* Boston, MA: Sigo Press.

Crosson-Tower, C. (1999). *Understanding Child Abuse and Neglect* (4th ed.). Boston, MA: Allyn and Bacon.

Crosson-Tower, C. (2002). *When Children are Abused. An Educator's Guide to Intervention.* Boston, MA: Allyn and Bacon.

Hardy, M. S. (2001). Physical Aggression and Sexual Behavior Among Siblings: A Retrospective Study. *Journal of Family Violence, 16*(3), 255–268.

Kelley, B. T., Thornberry, T. P., & Smith, C. A. (1997). *In the Wake of Childhood Maltreatment.* Washington, DC: U.S. Department of Justice. Office of Justice Programs. Office of Juvenile Justice and Delinquency Prevention (NCJ-165257).

Klosinski, G. (1993). Psychological Maltreatment in the Context of Separation and Divorce. *Child Abuse and Neglect, 17*(4), 557–563.

McCabe, K. A. (2000). Child Pornography and the Internet. *Social Science Computer Review, 18*(1), 73–76.

McCabe, K. A., & Gregory, S. S. (1997). *The Nature of South Carolina Violent Crime.* Columbia, SC: S.C. Dept. of Public Safety. Office of Safety and Grants.

Miedzian, M. (1995). Learning to Be Violent. In E. Peled, P.G. Jaffe & J. L. Edelson (eds.) *Ending the Cycle of Violence: Community Responses to Children of Battered Women.* Thousand Oaks, CA: Sage, pp. 10–24.

O' Hagan, K. (1993). *Emotional and Psychological Abuse of Children.* Toronto: University of Toronto Press.

Sedlak, A. J. & Broadhurst, D. D. (1996). *Executive Summary of the Third National Incidence Study of Child Abuse and Neglect. National Clearinghouse on Child Abuse and Neglect Information.* Washington, DC: U.S. Department of Health and Human Services. The Administration for Children and Families. National Center on Child Abuse and Neglect (ACF-1059418).

Wallace, H. (1999). *Family Violence. Legal, Medical, and Social Perspectives* (2nd ed.). Boston, MA: Allyn and Bacon.

Wiehe, V. R. (1997). *Sibling Abuse. Hidden Physical, Emotional, and Sexual Trauma* (2nd ed.). Thousand Oaks, CA: Sage.

Wolfe, D. A., Wekerle, C., Reitzel-Jaffe, D., Grasley, C., Pittman, A. & MacEachran, A. (1997). Interrupting the Cycle of Violence: Empowering Youth to Promote Healthy Relationships. In D. A. Wolfe, R. J. McMahan & R. D. Peters (eds.) *Child Abuse: New Directions in Prevention and Treatment Across the Lifespan.* Thousand Oaks, CA: Sage, pp. 102–129.

Chapter 5

Administration for Children and Families [ACF]. (1999). 1999 National Child Abuse and Neglect Reporting System. Highlights of Findings. Washington, DC: U.S. Department of Health and Human Services. http://www.acf.dhhs.gov/programs/cb/publications/cm99/high.html accessed January 20, 2001.

Barkan, S. E. (2001). *Criminology. A Sociological Understanding* (2nd ed.). Upper Saddle River, NJ: Prentice Hall.

Bartollas, C. (2000). *Juvenile Delinquency* (5th ed.). Boston, MA: Allyn and Bacon.

Bynum, J. E. & Thompson, W. E. (2002). *Juvenile Delinquency: A Sociological Approach* (5th ed.). Boston, MA: Allyn and Bacon.

Crosson-Tower, C. (1999). *Understanding Child Abuse and Neglect* (4th ed.). Boston, MA: Allyn and Bacon.

Crosson-Tower, C. (2002). *When Children are Abused. An Educator's Guide to Intervention.* Boston, MA: Allyn and Bacon.

English, P.C. (1978). Failure to Thrive Without Organic Reason. *Pediatric Annals, 7*, 774–780.

Gabarino, J. & Collins, C. C. (1999). Child Neglect: The Family with the Hole in the Middle. In H. Dubowitz (ed.) *Neglected Children: Research, Practice, and Policy.* Thousand Oaks, CA: Sage, pp. 1–23.

Gaudin, J. M. (1993). *Child Neglect: A Guide for Intervention.* Washington, DC: U.S. Department of Health and Human Services. Administration for Children and Families. (HHS-105891730).

Helfer, R. E. & Kempe, R. S. (1987). *The Battered Child* (4th ed.). Chicago, IL: University of Chicago Press.

Higham, S. & Horwitz, S. (2001). Family Sues over Foster Child's Death: $120 Million Case Alleges Negligence and Abusing by D.C., Delaware Nursing Home. *The Washington Post,* B2, November 28.

Kelley, B. T., Thornberry, T. P., & Smith, C. A. (1997). *In the Wake of Childhood Maltreatment.* Washington, DC: U.S. Department of Justice. Office of Justice Programs. Office of Juvenile Justice and Delinquency Prevention (NCJ-165257).

National Center on Child Abuse and Neglect [NCCAN]. 1993. *Child Neglect: A Guide for Intervention.* Washington, DC: U.S. Department of Health and Human Services. Administration for Children and Families (HHS-105891730).

Omaha World Herald. (2002). City Looks for Children as Omaha Law Aims at Cracking Down on Leaving Kids Alone in Cars. *Editorial,* 8B, May 26.

Pelzer, D. (1995). *A Child Called It.* Deerfield, FL: Health Communications, Inc.

Sedlak, A. J. & Broadhurst, D. D. (1996). *Executive Summary of the Third National Incidence Study of Child Abuse and Neglect. National Clearinghouse on Child Abuse and Neglect Information.* Washington, DC: U.S. Department of Health and Human Services. The Administration for Children and Families. National Center on Child Abuse and Neglect (ACF-1059418).

Sudermann, M. & Jaffe, P. (1997). Children and Youth Who Witness Violence. In D. A. Wolfe, R. J. McMahon, & R. D. Peters (eds.) *Child Abuse. New Directions in the Prevention and Treatment Across the Lifespan.* Thousand Oaks, CA: Sage, pp. 55–78.

Wallace, H. (1999). *Family Violence. Legal, Medical, and Social Perspectives* (2nd ed.). Boston, MA: Allyn and Bacon.

Wolfe, D. A., McMahon, R. J., & Peters, R. D. (1997). *Child Abuse. New*

Directions in Prevention and Treatment Across the Lifespan. Thousand Oaks, CA: Sage.

Chapter 6

Bakan, D. (2001). Slaughter of the Innocents: A Study of the Battered Child Phenomenon. *Journal of Social Distress and the Homeless, 10*(2), 147–216.

Barkan, S. E. (2001). *Criminology. A Sociological Understanding* (2nd ed.). Upper Saddle River, NJ: Prentice Hall.

Berliner, L. (1997). Trauma-Specific Therapy for Sexually Abused Children. In D. Wolfe, R. McMahon & R. Peters (eds.) *Child Abuse. New Directions in Prevention and Treatment Across the Lifespan.* Thousand Oaks, CA: Sage, pp. 177–204.

Briere, J. (1997). Treating Adults Severely Abused as Children. In D. Wolfe, R. McMahon & R. Peters (eds.) *Child Abuse. New Directions in Prevention and Treatment Across the Lifespan.* Thousand Oaks, CA: Sage, pp. 177–204.

Brooks, W. & Weathers, L. (2001). The Shaken Baby Syndrome: A Multidisciplinary Approach. *Journal of Aggression, Maltreatment and Trauma, 5*(1), 1–8.

Child Abuse and Neglect State Statutes Elements. (2000A). Reporting Laws, No. 6. Penalties for Failure to Report. Washington, DC: National Clearinghouse on Child Abuse and Neglect.

Child Abuse and Neglect State Statutes Elements. (2000B). Reporting Laws, No. 9. Penalties for Failure to Report. Washington, DC: National Clearinghouse on Child Abuse and Neglect.

Crosson-Tower, C. (1999). *Understanding Child Abuse and Neglect* (4th ed.). Boston, MA: Allyn and Bacon.

Crosson-Tower, C. (2002). *When Children are Abused. An Educator's Guide to Intervention.* Boston, MA: Allyn and Bacon.

Davies, W. H. & Garwood, M. W. (2001). Who are the Perpetrators and Why Do They Do It? *Journal of Aggression, Maltreatment, and Trauma, 5*(1), 41–54.

Finkelhor, D. (1984). *Child Sexual Abuse. New Theories and Research.* New York, NY: Free Press.

Finkelhor, D. & Ormrod, R. (2001). *Child Abuse Reported to the Police.* Washington, DC: U.S. Department of Justice. Office of Justice Programs: Office of Juvenile Justice and Delinquency Prevention (OJJDP) (NCJ-187238).

Hagemann-White, C. (2001). European Research on the Prevalence of Violence Against Women. *Violence Against Women, 7*(7), 732–759.

Helfer, R. E. & Kempe, R. S. (1987). *The Battered Child* (4th ed.). Chicago, IL: University of Chicago Press.

Kapur, N. (2001). Equality and the Truth of Brahma. *Violence Against Women, 7*(9), 1069–1096.

Maxwell, C., Garner, J., & Fagan, J. (2001). *The Effects of Arrest on Intimate Partner Violence: New Evidence from the Spouse Assault Replication Program.* Washington, DC: U.S. Department of Justice. Office of Justice Programs. National Institute of Justice (NCJ-188199).

McCabe, K. A. (2000). Child Pornography and the Internet. *Social Science Computer Review, 18*(1), 73–76.

McCabe, K. A. & Lee, M. D. (1997). Users' Perceptions of Internet Regulation: An Exploratory Study. *Social Science Computer Review, 15*(3), 237–241.

McManis, S. (2002). Confessions Could Save Other Babies. Teen Mom Admits She Killed Newborn. *The San Francisco Chronicle,* A19, May 26.

Orbach, Y. & Lamb, M. E. (1999). Assessing the Accuracy of a Child's Account of Sexual Abuse: A Case Study. *Child Abuse and Neglect, 23*(1), 91–98.

Reid, S. T. (1995). *Criminal Law* (3rd ed.). Upper Saddle River, NJ: Prentice Hall.

Wallace, H. (1999). *Family Violence. Legal, Medical, and Social Perspectives* (2nd ed.). Boston, MA: Allyn and Bacon.

Index

GENERAL EDITORS
David A. Schultz & Christina DeJong

Studies in Crime and Punishment is a multidisciplinary series that publishes scholarly and teaching materials from a wide range of methodological perspectives and explores sentencing and criminology issues from a single nation or comparative perspective. Subject areas to be addressed in this series include, but will not be limited to: criminology, sentencing and incarceration, policing, law and the courts, juvenile crime, alternative sentencing methods, and criminological research methods.

For additional information about this series or for the submission of manuscripts, please contact:

David A. Schultz
Peter Lang Publishing
Acquisitions Department
275 Seventh Avenue, 28th floor
New York, New York 10001

To order other books in this series, please contact our Customer Service Department:

(800) 770-LANG (within the U.S.)
(212) 647-7706 (outside the U.S.)
(212) 647-7707 FAX

Or browse online by series:
www.peterlangusa.com